eucharist
with a
small
"e"

eucharist
with a
small
"e"

miriam therese winter

ORBIS BOOKS

Maryknoll, New York 10545

Founded in 1970, Orbis Books endeavors to publish works that enlighten the mind, nourish the spirit, and challenge the conscience. The publishing arm of the Maryknoll Fathers and Brothers, Orbis seeks to explore the global dimensions of the Christian faith and mission, to invite dialogue with diverse cultures and religious traditions, and to serve the cause of reconciliation and peace. The books published reflect the views of their authors and do not represent the official position of the Maryknoll Society. To learn more about Maryknoll and Orbis Books, please visit our website at www.maryknoll.org.

Library of Congress Cataloging-in-Publication Data

Winter, Miriam Therese.
    Eucharist with a small "e" / Miriam Therese Winter.
       p. cm.
    ISBN-13: 978-1-57075-617-7 (pbk.)
    1. Lord's Supper. 2. Sacred meals. 3. Dinners and dining – Religious aspects – Christianity. 4. Ritual. I. Title.
    BV825.3.W56 2005
    248.4′6 – dc22

                                         2005010656

To all of you
who encouraged me
to speak
about these things

Contents

Contents

PART THREE
Celebrating eucharist with a small "e"
Opening Up to the Spirit

Jesus and Meals

Preface

This book is not for those who prefer the methodology of scholars. There are no footnotes, no bibliographies, no carefully reasoned theories supported by cogent arguments that one might expect to see with regard to a book about eucharist.

This is a book for people in the pews and for people who have left the pews yet long for something sacramental. It is not for Catholics only, although some sections of the book are from a Catholic perspective.

A small book with a big agenda, *eucharist with a small "e"* promotes a deeper integration of the sacred and the secular, sees the basic realities of life as elements of eucharist, and invites the world to join in celebrating the liturgy of life. Its basic presupposition is: whatever nurtures and nourishes faith, or the ever resilient wellsprings of hope, or gives rise to the manifold facets of love is potentially eucharist.

This message unfolds within a framework that celebrates God's word as embodied word and, therefore, as sacrament. Selected stories from scripture, both parables and Gospel narratives, are told from the perspective of a storyteller, not a chronicler. This means that a literal retelling of the texts is not how the stories are told again here. Instead, as teller caught up in a theme, I tried to tell the story in a way that might have some relevance for us, with the hope that this might kindle a response or in some way speak to the heart. Within our textual tradition, such a retelling is called a paraphrase, yet in the ancient oral tradition where storytellers were the norm, this more fluent mode of transmission is legitimate and authentic. This does not mean these scriptural stories were given a contemporary setting. It does mean that in a number of instances the distance between their time and ours might seem easier to transcend. As each of us tells these stories in turn within a communal context, we may more easily discern what their ancient wisdom is saying to us now; and as we dis-cover points of application and connection to our own lives, perhaps we will feel free to add an interpretation of our own.

Telling tradition's stories is understood to be preliminary to the telling of our own, for the stories embedded in scripture were once the lived reality of people just like us. Only when we make this connection will we see that there was, once upon a time, a period of oral transmission when even the most sacred of our stories were open to variation and improvisation as they were told and retold. As our own stories emerge, it is hoped that we will recognize that we are the continuation of generations past who told God's sacred story in their own time and place. Only then will we understand what it is really like not to be bound by syllables on a page. We may even speak of a Third Testament in its oral stages, guided by the Spirit, prodding us and inspiring us to wrestle with and respond to the challenges of our times.

Eucharist with a small "e" is a lens that will eventually filter how and what we see. Over time we may well shift positions on what we exclude and what we embrace. This much is cer-tain to many of us: we need a new lens that refracts a wider and more empathetic understanding of the world in which we live, one that will bring into sharper focus the Spirit-led role we are to play in an ever-expanding universe. We can see to the edge of the universe now but remain strangely captivated by a world of our own making. Yet we must look beyond it, look long and hard into our own souls for the soft underbelly of mercy, face the dividing lines of our differences, the restrictions of our religiosity, the confines of our canons, the precipice of our prejudices, and dare to step across the chasm to experience the other side. That is what Jesus did. The stories that are in this book tell us how and why.

Acknowledgments

The principal scriptural resource used in this book is the New Revised Standard Version Bible, copyright © 1993 by the Division of Christian Education of the National Council of the Churches of Christ in the U.S.A. Punctuation of quotations is often intentionally unconventional.

The brief citations introducing each chapter in Part Three are taken from songs written by the author. Most of these appear in the anthology entitled *Songlines*. For more information about music and books by Miriam Therese Winter, please visit *http://mtwinter.hartsem.edu.*

PART ONE

Acknowledging eucharist with a small "e"

~⌾~

In and through the Spirit

~ 1 ~

A new way of seeing

Do you see what I see? That is what this book is about. Come, see what I see, another way of understanding and celebrating eucharist.

The spirit and vision of Jesus as expressed through his relationship to the God of his experience and to the world around him are the underlying spirit and vision of eucharist with a small "e." Imagine a spirituality rooted in doing what Jesus did, one that adds a sacramental dimension to our everyday lives. Such a spiritual practice in which there is shared leadership and immediate relevance will inevitably lead to a growing awareness of our responsibility to continue the mission and ministries of Jesus in our times.

This book is not about the Sacrament of the Eucharist but about a parallel practice within Christian tradition. Eucharist with a small "e" goes all the way back to Jesus and is a vital part of our Christian heritage. From the earliest days of the apostolic church, this genuine eucharistic practice has sustained countless communities of faith. It has the capacity to speak to us now, to nourish us and transform us. What follows is an invitation to retrieve this authentic tradition from the shadows of our received Tradition and let the spirit of Jesus into our frenzied, fragmented lives.

What do we do between Sundays? How do we learn to live responsibly and with integrity? There is an innate longing today for a spirituality of the spirit of Jesus to permeate all aspects of the troubled world in which we live. The challenge will be to see, really see, what is right before our eyes, to see that ways of embracing and embodying the spirit of Jesus are literally everywhere.

Celebrating eucharist with a small "e" will expand the way we see the world, and that can make all the difference. Its purpose is not to celebrate a sacrament but to live sacramentally. The underlying ethos of this book is to help us see the substance of our story and the stuff of our lives as eucharist.

Eucharist with a small "e" is presented not as a substitute for the Sacrament of the Eucharist or as an alternative to it but as coexistent with it. To celebrate eucharist with a small "e" requires no permission, breaks no law. There is no prerequisite training needed nor any expertise. It is a legitimate option arising from a sincere desire for spiritual innerconnectedness with God and with one another, and it is open to everyone.

– 2 –

A sacramental journey

I first encountered the God of my tradition, not through organized religion, but in the freewheeling world of the spirit. God was there in the magic and the mystery of every new discovery and literally meant the world to me before I understood the mystical meaning of that claim.

We communicated without inhibition, I with a child's acceptance of everything that is real, which included that which the eye cannot see and the One Unseen with an eagerness to be made manifest. Trees, stars, wind, woods, berries, birdsong, bubbling brook were my first sacred texts. God's creation was my sanctuary, where I celebrated rites and rituals that strengthened my relationship with the One who had created me. Long meandering walks in the summer and silent vigils beneath the stars taught me more about the Divine than any curriculum. Through poems that I began to write at a very early age, I imagined the One in Whom I lived and from Whom I received my being. Communion with God was direct and personal, free of theological overlays or complex interpretations. That was the way it was before I reached the age of reason, when the institutional church stepped in to teach me all about God.

I remember the day I received the Eucharist for the very first time, or, as we Catholics prefer to say, when I made my First Communion. I was dressed in white from head to toe and I looked and felt like an angel. I was given a brand new rosary and a new prayer book with colorful illustrations, which I put into my tiny white purse and carried everywhere.

I was eager to receive Jesus, yet secretly I was afraid, for they said he would be coming to me in the form of a small, dry wafer that would be difficult to swallow. What if it stuck to the roof of my mouth? We had been warned time and again never to touch the Host with our fingers, and if it should stick to the roof of our mouth, well then, just leave it there. That did not relieve my anxiety. The Communion wafer was not an "it," but really and truly Jesus. What if I had to walk around for days with Jesus stuck to the roof of my mouth? I didn't tell anyone about my fear, but I did ask God to help me. Please God, I prayed, let Jesus not be too hard for me to swallow. Mercifully, God obliged, and my prayer continues to be answered, on a theological level, even to this day.

Sacramental Communion left me substantially changed. Although I was only seven years old, I knew and understood that Jesus loved little children and that Jesus had come to me. I also knew that Jesus would always be there for me, that he was now and would always be an essential part of my life. My encounter with Jesus in the Eucharist added another dimension to my spiritual awakening. It introduced me to religion.

Obligatory Sunday Mass was not an obligation for me, for I liked the sound of the Latin language, the sense of mystery it conveyed, the meaning I gleaned as I read the texts translated for me in my Missal. I went to Mass and Communion daily and fervently participated in many other devotional rituals: exposition of the Blessed Sacrament, Benediction, Forty Hours, Stations of the Cross, novenas, the May crowning of the Virgin Mary as Queen of Heaven and Earth. I wore her scapular, prayed the rosary, made visits to church at various times to sit quietly with Jesus, lit votive candles for special needs, honored the nine First Fridays, fasted during Lent, never ate meat on Friday, filled my bedroom with pictures of the Sacred Heart of Jesus, Jesus the Good Shepherd, the Risen Christ, the One who stands at the door and knocks. I ransomed pagan babies for Christ through Propaganda Fide, became a member of the parish choir and the Sodality, and was involved in two major movements, Catholic Action and Crusade for Christ.

Growing up Catholic also meant being shaped by ecclesiastical canons. Eager to be a good Catholic, I accepted the rules and the rubrics with unquestioning allegiance. It never occurred to me that the church's dogmatic expectations did not coincide with my earlier and equally formative experience of the sacred. The God I knew before I knew about God was still an integral part of me and continued to reach out to and into me through everything around me. This God of my childhood faith seemed content to let me be me without having to make me over and never once presented me with a list of unequivocal demands. On the other hand, the God of my religious affiliation was sometimes quite demanding. Nevertheless, I was blessed by both my worlds, the outer one shaped by religion and my inner world of the spirit, where I felt creative and free. At that young age I was too naïve to perceive the paradox inherent in following both these paths.

Automatically, effortlessly, I began to inhabit two worlds, the world of the church's expectations and the world of my inner spirit. I retreated to this inner world in between other activities, secretly writing poems that at times were theological explorations, but more often the unabridged outpourings of a child's uninitiated heart. In this safe and sacred space, I could dream and I could imagine. I cherished the freedom to do this unrestricted and unafraid. This parallel universe co-existed alongside the realities of daily life. In the world where everyone else was, I behaved as was expected and stayed within the lines. In the parallel world of the spirit, and I speak here of a spiritual life, it was at times exhilarating and always liberating, because I related to God and to life in a completely different way. My spirit danced between both worlds for all the years that followed. It dances between them still.

As I entered into adolescence, I was able to integrate my perception of God's real presence everywhere with the church's sacramental understanding of Christ's Real Presence in the Eucharist, although it was never a conscious effort to reconcile the two. I believed in the Real Presence of Jesus. I wanted to spend time with him within me after receiving Communion, giving thanks for his many blessings, seeking direction, interceding for others, or simply sitting in silence. Through Communion and through hearing his story in the Gospels at Mass, I came to know Jesus. However, it was through the church's teachings that I came to know Jesus as God.

A change of address and changes in me during my early teens eventually tempered my religious fervor. High school was compelling. I relished the classes, both elective and required, the extracurricular activities, which included a coveted spot on the varsity cheerleading squad, and just hanging out with my friends.

There were ample opportunities to consider a career path, higher education, even being married with children. However, a call to another way was deep and ultimately persuasive. Just before graduation, I set the course for my future by declaring I would enter religious life. Although what lay ahead was completely unknown, there was certainty in the call. I was led by the Spirit to a community of women called Medical Mission Sisters, an international, multicultural congregation committed to ministries of health and healing all around the world.

At the motherhouse in Philadelphia, my outer and inner worlds grew to be complementary. There was structure in the order of the day, in the prayers and the work and the discipline, and there was also freedom, if one knew where to look for it. I found it in the silences, in the acres of fields and orchards, in the small wooded areas teeming with birds and butterflies, in the large public parks adjacent to our property, in the rain and the wind and the stars. Here I experienced a more intense immersion into Eucharist through liturgy and the liturgical year and an intentional liturgical life. Living the liturgy day after day, season after season, taught me how to weave into one the liturgical and secular seasons and the seasons of the heart. Such a deep integration of life's fundamental rhythms released within me a sense of gratitude resonant with Spirit, revealing a dimension of the Divine that would eventually transform me. Now and then my heart aches to return again to that space and time when ordinary, everyday life was rendered quintessentially sacred, a perspective that, in these latter days, continues to elude us.

After my profession of vows, I earned a degree in liturgical music and returned to the motherhouse with an expertise that was superfluous, for the ancient rites were changing. Vatican II had stripped them of generations of accretions, bequeathing to the Eucharist primacy of place at the core of a vernacular liturgy now radically reformed. The biggest challenge facing our transition from Latin to English was the paucity of singable songs. It is here that my spirit world broke through to influence and shape my external life. I began giving birth to biblically based songs, a different kind of liturgical song, to bring life into the liturgy and the liturgy into life, thereby crossing a threshold into a unifying place where my bifurcated worlds were one. It took a while for me to grow into the person I was becoming. Over time I came to appreciate the importance of speaking aloud that which I believe the Spirit would have me see and say. The evolution from secretly writing poems to publicly singing songs advocating justice and peace and love was a personal metamorphosis of cosmic proportions. From that moment on, in significant ways, I began to change.

The shifts in perception and perspective that have honed me in the intervening years inherently shape this volume. I believe Jesus says to every age through his active, activating Spirit: "I am making all things new" (Rev 21:5). That word from the past reverberates now with renewed intensity. We need new ways of thinking, new ways of being and behaving in a world swiftly spinning out of control. We need new sources of leadership, an infusion of new energy, a faith for a new millennium that is oriented to the future instead of the past. We especially need to purge ourselves of attitudes and actions that have nothing to do with Jesus and do not reflect the liberating word he would have us preach in his name.

Eucharist with a small "e" will help us to evoke the perspective of Jesus within traditional religion, for it does not happen apart from life but right in the midst of it. It prepares us and conditions us to see life itself as sacred, empowers us to take responsibility for making a difference in our world, provides a vehicle for counting our blessings and a time for giving thanks. For those of us who want to be shaped by the vision and spirit of Jesus, it is in fact a sacramental journey into the heart of God.

~ 3 ~

The origins of eucharist

Eucharist in Christian tradition originated with Jesus. He is its primary source and ongoing inspiration. Two distinctive paradigms for the theology and practice of eucharist flow from the life and spirit of Jesus. The one that is most familiar to us, the Sacrament of the Eucharist, evolved from the table fellowship of the followers of Jesus after he had died. The other, eucharist with a small "e," is reflected in the experiences of Jesus eating and drinking with others while he was still alive. The resurrection meals are a link between the two. A brief consideration of the origins of our traditional Eucharist will provide the context for introducing eucharist with a small "e."

Most Christians have grown up convinced that Jesus celebrated the First Eucharist at the Last Supper. Our mental image of the event has Jesus sitting at a table with his male disciples. He is holding a cup and a host in his hands and is gazing heavenward. For Catholics this is the First Mass, yet the reality was quite different. That final meal of Jesus, and much of what we regard as factual concerning Christian origins, has been framed by art and interpretation, by piety and preaching, and by an ever-evolving tradition.

Jesus did not celebrate Eucharist on the night before he died. Not in the way that we understand it. Jesus was not a Christian. He lived and died a Jew. His final meal took place prior to Christianity, in a Jewish context, during a Passover festival. The Eucharist of Christian tradition emerged after Jesus was gone as a way of remembering him, for his life and his living spirit had inspired the birth of a movement in his memory and his name.

If the Last Supper was not the First Mass, then where did the sacrament originate? In some sense, paradoxically, at that same supper, for that was the genesis of its ethos and its energy. The empowering presence of the person and the passionate spirit of Jesus at that decisive moment transcended the confines of historic fact and continued to live on. What exactly happened that night? We can only speculate, for the evidence is inconclusive. We do know that a traditional blessing on a traditionally festive occasion was lifted out of the ordinary and invested with an extraordinary power to transfix and transform. What Jesus said and did during their last time together lived on in the hearts of his followers after he had died. When they gathered to remember, they struggled to understand the meaning of his words, the implications of his images and symbolic associations, the challenge of loving passionately, his promise of an abiding spirit. The seeds of a future Eucharist that were sown during that memorable night would soon germinate and spread far beyond his inner circle. It wasn't long before Eucharist took on a life of its own. How and when did the Eucharist assume the characteristically Christian form with which we are now familiar? For this phase of development, we turn to the apostle Paul.

Paul and the community in Corinth

Paul was a Pharisaic Jew whose conversion to Christianity shocked the nascent church. Many knew firsthand how relentless he had been in persecuting Christians in Jerusalem, how he had gone from house to house executing a purge against followers of the Way. He was bound for Damascus with a similar intent when his prejudice was suddenly overturned by a heavenly intervention. Confronted with his blindness, he was led to see the light, and his subsequent influence, theological and otherwise, on the church he now embraced as his own has been truly monumental. Paul spent the rest of his life proclaiming Christ to the Gentiles and facilitating the formation of Christian communities abroad. It is ironic that Paul, who had never known Jesus and was not an eyewitness to either his death or his resurrection, is responsible for the unique way we celebrate Eucharist today.

To understand precisely what this means, let us go to Corinth, an urban center in the Greco-Roman world, where Paul had settled for a time and was actively advancing the Christian cause. Corinth was a pagan society whose citizens reflected a spectrum of religious and cultural contexts that represented diverse customs and beliefs. Add to this panorama the additional perspectives of female and male, rich and poor, and you have a sense of the church in Corinth. The fact that there was dissension should come as no surprise. There were even competing factions as the number of house-churches increased, as well as issues concerning their sacramental meal.

Paul had reason to worry about the integrity of that meal. Some Christians were still making sacrificial offerings to pagan gods. As converts, they lacked the cultural context to com-prehend what it meant to proclaim that Jesus died, yet lives. Sometimes the festivity of their meals got a bit out of hand. Yes, resurrection is incredibly good news, but there was first a crucifixion with implications for all. There was also the clash of a socioeconomic disparity. While Christian ideology in-sisted that all the members are one, their common meal said otherwise, for some had more and some had less, and others at times had nothing. Deeply entrenched divisions, no matter how passionate the piety, are not so easily dispelled.

While he was away, Paul sent several letters expressing his concerns. Vital to our understanding of the evolution of Chris-tian Eucharist are chapters 10 through 14 in the first of his letters to the community in Corinth.

Paul explains that to break bread together means one is part of the body of Christ; therefore pagan sacrifice is something to be abhorred. He reprimands the community for what he considers unacceptable behavior, for when they come together as church to celebrate Eucharist as part of their meal, they do not always eat together or share food with one another. On the other hand, Paul is lyrical in his description of the collective gifts of the Spirit manifested within the community, insisting that each one's gift is valued and that all have equal worth. He writes eloquently of love, expresses his opinion on speaking in tongues, and then concludes with an order of worship that reflects liturgical form and function in Corinth's multicultural context.

We learn from this letter, a primary source regarding early Christian worship, that in Corinthian liturgy there was active involvement of those present, shared leadership through the

sharing of gifts, variety and spontaneity. Anyone could contribute to the worship experience as inspired by the Spirit,
according to the gift each had been given. Paul did insist that
all be done with a sense of decency and order, for the point
of all participation was to build community. This valuable
source of information from the earliest days of the apostolic church reveals that liturgical worship was adapted to
local contexts and allowed for freedom of expression within
a loosely structured format. It provides an essential link in
tracing the development of the eucharistic rite.

Paul's unique contribution to the liturgical shape and theological thrust of Eucharist in Western Christianity is recorded
in 1 Corinthians 11:23–26. He writes:

> For I received what I also handed on to you, that Jesus on
> the night when he was betrayed took a loaf of bread, and
> when he had given thanks, he broke it and said, "This
> is my body that is for you. Do this in remembrance of
> me." In the same way he took the cup also, after supper,
> saying, "This cup is the new covenant in my blood. Do
> this as often as you drink it, in remembrance of me."
> For as often as you eat this bread and drink the cup, you
> proclaim the death of Jesus until he comes.

These ancient words, so familiar to us, define Eucharist. To
some they include words of institution that evoke the Real
Presence of Christ in the Roman Catholic Mass. To others
they are words of warrant for the sacrament's symbolic action. Because of their setting in the life of faith, it is difficult
to appreciate the historical significance of the text in which
these words are embedded, but it is critical that we do so.

Recorded here are decisive contributions to the development of the Eucharist that have been attributed to Paul.

With his reference to the night when Jesus was betrayed, Paul links the sacramental meal of the Corinthian community with the Last Supper, thereby establishing an ontological connection between the two. He is the first to make this explicit association. The breaking of the bread by Jesus the Jew on the night before he died is now a Christian tradition; the cup is sign of a new covenant sealed in Christ's blood. This is a radical reorientation of existing understanding. What would become our traditional form of celebrating Eucharist originated with Paul.

Paul shifts the focus of attention to the elements of the eucharist, to the bread and to the cup. The words that were spoken by Jesus in reference to his body and blood are placed in parallel relationship by Paul precisely for ritual use. In addition they are invested with a meaning that could hardly have originated with Paul. It is far too early to suggest that the explicit location of Christ's presence in the eucharist is in the bread and the wine. At this stage of development, the presence of Christ is in the community gathered to share a meal. When they eat and drink together and enjoy fellowship together, Christ is truly present, transforming the community into the body of Christ. This too is a decisive Pauline contribution to theological understanding. To break bread is to be part of the extended body of Christ, for all who partake of the one bread are one body. That is why Paul is so concerned about appropriate behavior. To treat one another unkindly or unjustly is to violate the body and incur divine wrath. What would become the words of institution — this is my body ... this is my blood — passed through a lengthy period of development before settling into the precise formulaic words of our traditional rites. In time these words were accorded primacy of place and set apart by canonical laws determining who might utter them and by a theological understanding of what they indeed effect.

In another distinctive contribution, Paul defines the meaning of the eucharist for the Corinthian community. He tells them that whenever they gather for this sacramental meal, they are proclaiming the death of Jesus until he returns again (11:26). This eucharistic meal for Paul is a type of memorial rite wherein the community assembles to remember both the death of Jesus and the coming of the messianic Christ. Remembering for Paul means far more than calling to mind a past event. It is a liturgical remembering, what liturgists call *anamnesis,* whereby the past is made present again in this time and in this place. This means that the power and the spirit and the grace of that past historic event is effective here and now in this community. Through such a remembering, the body of believers and the body of Christ are one in the blood of a new covenant, the blood of the one who died and whose death gives life. This understanding is central to eucharistic theology, and we owe this development to Paul.

Perhaps to make the celebration of eucharist normative in the growing number of churches, there is an added instruction, which is, to "do this in remembrance of me." These words have been attributed to Jesus. However, there is consensus that these may not be the words of Jesus, but rather a rubric that arose either from one of the first communities or specifically from Paul, and that it was probably added to ensure the rite's repetition.

By what authority does Paul impose his personal interpretations on our eucharistic rite? As if anticipating our question, he tells us that he is handing on what has been revealed to him (11:23). From that revelation he concludes that the eucharistic community is the body of Christ proclaiming Christ's death until he comes again.

It is important to recall that the document that includes the texts analyzed in this chapter was written in reaction to a troublesome situation that was local and therefore limited. How much was meant to apply only to those particular problems in that particular place we will never really know. Paul wrote to correct abuses arising from an immature understanding in the Corinthian church. In any response to a specific concern there is always danger of overstatement and an overreaction. Nevertheless, what Paul wrote was given universal application and gained widespread acceptance. His words, once published, took on a life of their own, significantly impacting the shape of the eucharist well beyond Corinth.

Paul was the first to document early Christian eucharist, both theology and practice, in Gentile territory. There was, however, an earlier experience also recorded in scripture, a very different experience among Palestinian Jews.

The community in Jerusalem

While Paul was still persecuting Christians prior to his conversion, the community in Jerusalem celebrated eucharist. Here

is how it has been described at the beginning of the Book
of Acts.

> They devoted themselves to the apostles' teaching and
> fellowship, to the breaking of bread and the prayers. Awe
> came upon everyone, because many wonders and signs
> were being done by the apostles. All who believed were
> together and had all things in common; they would sell
> their possessions and goods and distribute the proceeds
> to all, as any had need. Day by day, as they spent much
> time together in the temple, they broke bread at home
> and ate their food with glad and generous hearts, prais-
> ing God and having the goodwill of all the people. And
> day by day many were added to those who were being
> saved. (2:42–47)

How very different, indeed, from what we know of Corinth.
The community in Jerusalem, outgrowth of a Spirit-charged
experience of Pentecost, prayed together and stayed together,
shared property and possessions, and supported with their surplus those who did not have enough. Women and men, slave
and free, rich and poor, young and old had thrown in their
lots together. They continued to go to the temple, for they
were observant Jews, and every day, together, they celebrated
eucharist.

What was this earliest eucharist like? It was an ordinary
meal that took place at home and it was characterized by a
spirit of enthusiastic joy. What was the reason behind this
joy at every communal meal? Surely not the memory of the
horrific death of Jesus, as Paul would later prescribe. Nobody
in Jerusalem, so soon after the crucifixion, would have found

any meaning in that. The death of Jesus was devastating. It had happened right there among them — the humiliation, the crucifying shame, the harsh brutality. They had been eye-witnesses, or were related to eyewitnesses, or had heard it told in excruciating detail time and time again. That cruel and painful memory was something they had tried to forget. The loss of one they had known and loved and had pinned their fragile hopes on was not a thing to celebrate. What could have been the source, then, of such a spirit of joy?

For Christians in Jerusalem, the death of Jesus was not the final chapter in his story. They had gone through all the emotions as their slain leader lay in the tomb, felt anguish, sorrow, disbelief, and, for a while, despair. Then one of the women insisted that she had seen Jesus. Other women said the same. The mood suddenly shifted. He is alive! He is still with us. He appeared to the community. He even ate with us. Yes, they had witnessed his suffering and death, but they were also eyewitnesses to his coming back to life.

The ecstatic, exuberant, euphoric joy that characterized their eucharist was rooted in the knowledge that Jesus, who died, had risen from the dead. That euphoria was evoked by the memory of recent meals where the Risen One appeared out of nowhere and proceeded to eat with them. The first resurrection appearance of Jesus to the disciples in community was in Jerusalem and it happened during a meal. Until he departed from their sight, they continued to encounter Jesus in the context of a meal.

Their initial joy in recalling those meals was accompanied by an intense experience of Jesus present among them when they came together at home for the breaking of bread.

Overjoyed, they knew he was still with them and would be present among them always at every communal meal. Soon, very soon, he would come again to fulfill his promise to them of a messianic banquet to be shared with him in glory. *Maranatha!* Come! This Aramaic invocation widespread in primitive Christianity meant a threefold coming, three ways of anticipating the presence of Christ: as the Risen One who had come to share a series of meals with them, as One who comes to be present among them in the breaking of the bread, as One who will come again in glory in the fullness of time. Dynamic. Expectant. *Maranatha!* Come!

The eucharist in Jerusalem is referred to in Acts as the breaking of bread. It is important to say again that this eucharist of the first Christians was an ordinary meal. In fact, the phrase "to break bread" usually meant "to take a meal." That meal itself consisted of whatever food happened to be served. In the process of eating and drinking together, of sharing memories, telling stories, interpreting the scriptures, articulating prayers, their fellowship was strengthened. There were no words of institution, no hint of anything associated with a collective participation in Christ's sacrificial death. Constitutive of this earliest eucharist was a resurrection spirit and an aura of hope. This shared experience of the presence of the risen Jesus in their midst was manifested in expressions of unmitigated joy.

Eucharist in the apostolic church

In summary, it can be said that two fundamentally different types of eucharist existed in the apostolic church.

The more primitive Jerusalem model described in the Book of Acts was celebrated in joyful anticipation of Christ's return in glory and was rooted in the memory of the community's post-Easter meals with Jesus.

The second, a Pauline corrective of the common meal in Corinth, proclaimed the death of Jesus in memory of that last supper on the night before he died.

Eucharist for both took place in the context of a meal. In Jerusalem this was known as the breaking of the bread. There was no mention of wine or cup, no formulaic ritual. Their experience of Christ present as they shared a meal together anticipated the promise of a messianic banquet when Christ would come again. At the sacramental supper in Corinth, participants became part of the body of Christ by eating and drinking together and experienced Christ's presence in the context of the meal and the sharing of the bread and the cup. The ritualized words that would evolve to become words of institution, together with a new theological thrust, took this model in the direction of a more formal, codified rite, a prototype of the Eucharist that predominates today. In those early decades of Christianity, the community ate *with* Christ; they did not eat Christ, who at this time was not seen as inhabiting the elements, although his presence at eucharist was real.

The distinction between the two types, one originating in the spirit of the resurrected Jesus, the other in remembrance of the crucified Christ, is palpable and profound. The ethos of each of these meals is substantially different, as is the manner of their celebration, and to some extent, their outcomes. The Corinthian model exhorts its members to focus on the body and blood of their crucified leader in memory of his death until his return, to realize they are now the body of Christ, and to act accordingly. The community in the Jerusalem model celebrates a meal with a loved one who is really present in spirit, having risen from the dead. Their communal bond is strengthened as they wait together in joyful anticipation of that which is to come.

— 4 —

Jesus:
eucharist with a small "e"

While Jesus is still in his mother's womb, an ecstatic cry of joy from her lips anticipates how history will define him. He fills the hungry with good things and sends the rich away empty. Indeed, it is the God of her tradition Mary praises in her *Magnificat*, but it is also a prophetic word that the mother-to-be is proclaiming. The child she carries will incarnate characteristics that empower the powerless and the poor and others who are oppressed. Long after he has come and gone, his spirit will continue to be there to satisfy those who hunger and thirst for justice and for mercy. This liberating spirit reaches out to us now from the very core of our everyday life. To become one with this spirit of Jesus is the purpose of eucharist with a small "e," which offers an itinerary for a sacramental journey that is available to everyone.

Let me put it bluntly, for good news needs to be heralded. Jesus *is* eucharist with a small "e." In Jesus the ancient *berakah* is the blessing of thanksgiving we call *eucharistia*. His presence among us in spirit energizes our own spirit to live as grace incarnate and to allow God's justice and compassion to be made manifest through us.

This is a *real* presence, a very real presence that sojourns among us in imaginative ways, proclaiming to and through us a word of wisdom to a war-weary world, a word of compassionate love.

Jesus is eucharist with a small "e" because he is the essence of its realization. Whenever and wherever we turn to Jesus to revivify the values he lived, we keep alive the vision that is now a vital force of Spirit poised to transform us all. We do this to proclaim God's love for all of God's creation. This is the good news that Jesus embodied, and we do this in memory of him.

Eucharist with a small "e" is not about rites or rituals. It is about relationship, about intensifying our relationship with God by immersing ourselves in the witness and wisdom of Jesus. To establish, and in time, to deepen a relationship with Jesus through our relationship with others and with the world around us is an essential outcome. The focus, therefore, is not on resources for prayer or coming up with an orderly design for a sacramental meal, but on developing those qualities that are relational, such as being genuinely hospitable, being a good listener, cultivating the gift of telling a story, beginning with one's own, encouraging others to tell their story, learning to share the concerns of the heart, sensing when Spirit is stirring, believing that the connections between eating and drinking and the spirit of Jesus are absolutely real.

Storytelling is characteristic of eucharist with a small "e." What we tell is essentially God's story through the story of Jesus and our own stories as they intersect and merge. The life of Jesus was a series of stories with deep roots in the real world before those flesh-and-blood events were reduced to

texts on a page. That did not happen for a while. His first
followers gathered to tell of their encounters and adventures
with Jesus, thereby recovering memories and exploring together the meaning of those memories for them. They relived
transformative moments in recalling the give and take of their
relationship with Jesus, and so can we. As we lift the underlying story of Jesus from the pages of our sacred texts, its
power and passion is once again transmitted to and through
us. Eucharist with a small "e" is all about story — the story of
God as it unfolds in the stories of Jesus, in our own stories,
and in the stories of our complicated world. In the lexicon of
eucharist with a small "e," story of God is the preferred way
of saying word of God because there is a tendency to separate word and sacrament. Our approach to words, even God's
word, is far too often didactic and therefore extremely limited.
Through eucharist with a small "e," we learn to see story *as*
sacrament and to celebrate the liturgy of life.

When we tell stories we become aware of things we had
previously overlooked. For example, the number of times food
is mentioned in the teachings of Jesus. That number is significant. Jesus taught his closest disciples to pray for daily bread
(Lk 11:3). He spoke consoling words to those whose circumstances seemed unlikely to change, promising those who were
hungry now that they would eat their fill, and then he warned
their oppressors who had plenty to eat that they would soon
be hungry (Lk 6:21, 25). When he sent his disciples out in
pairs like laborers to reap the harvest, he charged them to
settle down in one place and to eat and drink what was provided, because that was their due (Lk 10:7). Once, in Gentile
territory, a woman desperately seeking help begged Jesus to

cast the demon out of her troubled daughter. They say that Jesus told her to let the children be fed first, for it is not fair to take their food and throw it to the dogs, but she came right back at him, saying that even the dogs under the table eat the children's crumbs (Mk 7:24–30). The woman got what she wanted, for her daughter was instantly healed.

Jesus knew exactly what his critics thought of him and his cousin, John the Baptist. It is reported that he said: John came neither eating nor drinking, and they say, he has a demon, while I come eating and drinking, and they say, look, a glutton and a drunkard, a friend of tax collectors and sinners! (Mt 11:18–19). Much of the agenda of Jesus was revealed in the context of a meal. How he ate, where he ate, and especially with whom he ate and what he sometimes did while present at a meal were often political statements intended as a critique of the elite or a challenge to the ruling class. Strict social and religious structures scrupulously separated those who belonged from those considered unclean, for a purity code determined who was acceptable to God. Jesus contradicted this conventional understanding with his subversive behavior. He understood that there is more to a meal than assuaging physical hunger. Seeds of systemic change are sown when there is a place at the table for persons and perspectives that custom or tradition would exclude.

What we do in life has consequences for what happens both here and in the hereafter. That was the message of Jesus and many wondered, who can be saved? It was insufficient, he insisted, to say that we ate and drank with you and we were out there in the crowd when you were teaching in our streets (Lk 13:26), for there is no free pass through the law, but all have to put into practice God's universal love. Then Jesus proclaimed his vision of an egalitarian feast:

> People will come from east and west, from north and south, and will eat in the household of God. Indeed, some are last who will be first, and some are first who will be last. (Lk 13:29–30)

Many stories told by Jesus and told by others about Jesus revolve around a meal, and those meals are a revelatory source of how we ought to behave. So much of what Jesus said and did took place in domestic and social contexts, not in religious settings. It is remarkable that we still hesitate to validate the table fellowship of Jesus as authentic eucharist. It is especially ironic that the sacrament meant to ensure that the memory and mission of Jesus would live on is focused on a meal at the end of his life and not on all those many meals that tell us more about who he was and what our mission should be.

For this reason eucharist with a small "e" turns to those moments in the life of Jesus that are on the road less traveled. There is something to be learned from the emphasis Jesus gave to food as metaphor for our lived reality and to all those occasions when he participated in a meal. There may well be a roadmap here to guide us on our journey through the perilous pitfalls that would deter us from seeking the path of the heart. Surely our lives will be fuller and richer if we embody eucharist by ritually linking the life of Jesus with our own daily lives. What happened when he sat at table, what happens when his spirit is at our tables, suggests a practice redolent with hope and begs to be explored.

PART TWO

Recovering eucharist with a small "e"

❧

A Very Real Presence

~ 5 ~

Meals in the parables of Jesus

Parables, core to the teaching of Jesus, are evocative stories that enlighten and instruct. The point they make is sometimes more subtle than what we might expect, for parables are stories with a twist. They are meant to be told with a storyteller's skill, and then mulled over and discussed. The teller, the telling, the one who hears, the context in which the story is told contribute to its implications for a given time and place. As we listen again to each of the fifteen parables presented here, we turn to the Spirit for insight and a rudimentary understanding, and we look to our own experience for ways to interpret and apply the unconventional wisdom hidden in its ancient storyline.

When you are invited

When you are invited to a wedding, don't take a seat ordinarily reserved for someone of significance, for you may be asked to relinquish that seat and, much to your chagrin, will have to find another. Rather, sit in an inconspicuous place. When the host arrives and sees you there, you may be asked to join those guests seated at the head table, an honor in the eyes of all. (Lk 14:8–10)

∽℘∼

This parable is usually approached as a lesson in humility. The final words, omitted above, make that specific point:

> For all who exalt themselves will be humbled, and those who humble themselves will be exalted. (14:11)

These lines represent a saying of Jesus, like a moral that is appended to the end of a story, in fact, to more than one story. They were probably not part of the original telling but an added interpretation. While the theme of humility is relevant, the point of this story is limited if we consider it exclusively through that lens. For instance, would our own seat selection be determined primarily by status, or are we more often inclined to sit next to someone we know and like, or to avoid interacting with a stranger, or mingling with someone very different from us, whom we would rather not have to talk to? Is making an entrance or seizing the spotlight normally a higher priority than cultivating a new relationship or strengthening an old one? What are the concerns that arise in us when invited to a public function? What opportunities await us? What values guide the way we behave when socializing away from home?

When you invite others

When you prepare a luncheon or dinner, don't just invite your relatives or friends or people who are wealthy, for you may

*receive an invitation in return and then you will be repaid.
Invite the disadvantaged, who cannot pay you back. Then
at the end of your time here on earth, you will receive your
reward. (Lk 14:12–14)*

༄

The issue here is hospitality and the breadth of its application.
How wide is our circle? Who do we welcome to our table?
How diverse is our network of friends? We will never get to
know one another, especially those who differ from us, unless
we sit down together in the context of a meal and tell one
another who we are and what kind of world we envision. Who
among our acquaintances has stepped across our threshold
and shared a meal with us with no expectation whatsoever of
having to do something for us in return? If we are quick to
delete from our Rolodex those who fail to reciprocate, we will
never get to experience the joy of gift-giving societies, which
graciously give to friends and strangers with no expectation
of return.

The banquet

*Someone planned a special banquet and many were invited.
At the appointed time, a servant was sent to all those who
had received an invitation. Come now, they were told, for
everything was ready, but they began to make excuses. The
first, who had bought a piece of land, had to go out and see it,
and therefore could not come. Another had bought five yoke
of oxen and could not wait to try them out, and for that
reason, could not come. Another had been recently married*

and most certainly could not come. The servant returned to the owner of the house, who was angry at what had occurred. Go into the streets, the servant was told. Invite the poor and those who are in any way disadvantaged. When that was done, there was still room to spare, so the servant was sent to the byways and lanes and outlying areas of town to entice those who were living there to come to this special banquet, so the host's house might be filled. Those who had been the intended guests were now no longer welcome.

(Lk 14:15–24)

The wedding garment

Heaven may be compared to a monarch who was planning a wedding banquet. Servants were sent to call those invited to the banquet, but they refused to come. Still other servants were sent to say that the meal had been prepared, that oxen and fat calves had been slaughtered, that everything was ready for the banquet to begin. Those invited made light of it. Each of them went their own way, one to a farm, another to a business, while still others seized the servants, mistreated them, and killed them. The monarch was enraged. Troops were sent to destroy the guilty and set fire to their city. The wedding feast was ready, but those who had been privileged guests had proven to be unworthy. Servants were sent out into the streets to invite people, both good and bad, to come to the wedding banquet, until the hall was filled. The host came in to greet everyone and saw that one of the guests had arrived without a wedding garment. How could anyone manage to enter without the proper attire? The guilty one did not know what to say. The host then ordered the attendants to apprehend the intruder, who was bound hand and foot and thrown into the darkness, for many are called, but few are chosen. (Mt 22:1–14)

၀ၔ၀

These two parables have a similar theme and probably evolved from a single source. A story told to make a point could easily be adapted to fit a variety of situations, which is true of folk tales and fairy tales and certainly true of the parables. The dinner story seems to be aimed at individuals and their choices. The wedding banquet has systemic implications and political overtones. It is important to realize that the parables had something to say to their times and that their message was usually subversive. The social and religious systems during the lifetime of Jesus were predetermined and exclusionary. Followers of Jesus knew who should have been at those meals and would not have easily understood how outcasts could have been invited. Christian tradition has set these parables in the context of the endtime, giving a sense of finality to being in and out of favor and hinting at who will not be present at heaven's messianic meal. What do these parables have to say to us and to our times?

The lost sheep

Which one of you with a hundred sheep, should you lose one of them, would not leave the ninety-nine in the wilderness to look for the one that is lost? And when it has been found, would you not carry it home on your shoulders, rejoicing all

*the way? And when you are home, would you not celebrate
with friends and neighbors, saying, rejoice with me, for I have
found my sheep that was lost? So too there will be more joy
in heaven over one sinner who repents than over ninety-nine
righteous persons who are already reconciled. (Lk 15: 3–7)*

The lost coin

*Which one of you with ten silver coins, should you lose one
of them, would not light a lamp and sweep the floor and thor-
oughly search throughout the house until the coin is found?
And when you find it, would you not celebrate with friends
and neighbors, saying, rejoice with me, for I have found the
coin I had lost? So too there is joy among the angels of God
over one sinner who repents. (Lk 15:8–10)*

∽

The fifteenth chapter of Luke opens with grumbling among
some Pharisees and scribes because tax collectors and sinners continue to come to Jesus, who is accused not only of
welcoming sinners but also of eating with them. These intro-
ductory words remind us that certain people are considered
by some to be beyond the reach of grace and that these are
the very people found in the company of Jesus. Not only does
he mingle with them. He also eats with them. This reference
to fellowship shared at meals is more than a passing com-
ment here, for in each of the three parables that make up the
rest of chapter fifteen there is in fact a meal. In the first two
parables, presented above, the sharing of food is not made
explicit, but it certainly is implied. Both the shepherd who

found the sheep that was lost and the one who recovered a lost coin call in their friends and neighbors to celebrate with them. Food and drink are givens at celebrations such as these. We know from experience. To invite people in to celebrate with you means there will be something to eat and drink, usually something special, and more than enough for all. In these two parables, something was lost and then it was found, giving rise to a shared celebration. What have we lost? What have we found? What do we long to celebrate? Who in the world around us is lost and needs to be reconnected? Who are the outsiders we might invite to take a place at our table? The following parable, the third in the series presented by Luke, gives rise to similar questions. It tells of a lost child who has been found and describes the thanksgiving celebration.

The prodigal

A family had two children. The younger one asked for a share of what was to have been their inheritance, and when the property had been divided and apportioned equally, left home for a distant land and behaved irresponsibly. The money was spent without restraint, and in no time at all it was gone. A devastating famine struck. Everyone was hungry. The prodigal fed a farmer's pigs in order to survive, longing to eat what those animals ate. One day there came an awakening. What am I doing living like this? Why am I dying of hunger here when there is food at home? Why not go back to my family and ask to be forgiven? The prodigal was still a long way off when someone shouted: look who is coming! Father and

*mother ran all the way to meet and greet their beloved child
with tears and warm embraces. Quick! Bring a robe! The
very best! Bring sandals and adornments! Catch and prepare
the fatted calf. Let us give thanks with a festive meal, for our
child who was dead is alive again. The one who was lost has
been found!*

*It was quite a celebration. The elder sibling came in from
the fields and heard the raucous music, the singing and the
dancing. The servants explained what was happening, how
the wanderer had come back to the fold and how all had
joined the festivities in thanksgiving for a safe return. The
firstborn was furious and refused to participate. Both parents
tried to intercede, but they were unsuccessful. Bitter words
revealed why their eldest was so resentful. All these years
I worked for you. I never disobeyed you. I never ran away
from home, yet you have not given me even a goat so I might
celebrate with my friends. But when this profligate child of
yours finally decides to come home, you kill the fatted calf!
Then the following words were said with sorrow and with
more than a little regret. Child, you are always with us, and
all that is ours is yours. But we had to celebrate and rejoice,
because one who is also our flesh and blood was dead and
now lives again, was lost and has been found. (Lk 15:11–32)*

~~~

No doubt it was startling to read that both mother and father ran to meet and embrace their returning child. And
isn't that unfortunate. Why would anyone be surprised to
find a mother in this picture? No, she is not mentioned in
the account recorded in scripture, but she surely was in the

backstory before the circulating tale settled into a textual form. From experience we know that a mother would run the fastest and the farthest to be the first to hold once again the beloved child of her womb. Listen and you will hear her ongoing influence in the story, scurrying to provide a robe and sandals and decorative adornments, making sure that the news spread far and wide so all would join in celebration, choosing the best as she arranged for a lavishly sumptuous and festive meal.

This third parable about lost and found has to do with people and is focused on a family. We need to pay attention, not only to what happens to one lost child, but to each family member who, at some point in the story, feels a deep sense of loss.

This familiar parable is a favorite of many, perhaps because we see ourselves somewhere in the story. It is about relation-ship, about coming to our senses with regard to priorities, not only for the prodigal child but for all members of the family. The word "prodigal" means an extravagance, both negative and positive. This is a story of prodigality, of wastefulness and generosity, of hostility and hospitality, of the pitfalls of licen-tiousness and of the lavishness of love. The centerpiece is a thanksgiving meal, which functions as a turning point on the way to a resolution. This story of leaving and return is ulti-mately one of reversal. In a certain sense it is unresolved. The elder sibling is unreconciled. Does finding one who was lost really mean having to lose another? The story does not end here. Perhaps we are meant to seek a resolution in our own storylines.

The good Samaritan

A traveler going down the road from Jerusalem to Jericho fell into the hands of a band of thieves and was stripped, beaten, and left to die. Now it happened that a priest going down that road ignored the one who was wounded and passed by on the other side. A Levite traveling the same road saw the broken body, and without breaking stride, passed by on the other side. A Samaritan approached the stranger lying along the side of the road, and filled with compassion, took time to tend to the victim's wounds and to transport the injured one to the shelter of an inn. The Samaritan remained there overnight to care for the one who had been assaulted and in the morning paid the innkeeper to do the same, saying, "On my return I will reimburse you for whatever else you spend." Which of these three, do you think, was neighbor to the unfortunate one who fell into the hands of thieves? (Lk 10:30–37)

੨୧୨

A lawyer in the crowd had asked Jesus, "Who is my neighbor?" This parable was his reply. In the story Jesus illustrates how the true neighbor would not allow the rubrics of restriction to take precedence over human need. Those who are expected to be paragons of giving good example are not, while the one who is forever outside the circle becomes the role model for all. The phrase "Good Samaritan" is pretty much a cliché in our society. There is even a law that supports and protects neighborly interventions. It is hard, therefore, for us to feel the full impact of what it meant for a Jew to call a Samaritan "good." The quintessential outsider shows by example how we ought to behave. At the end of the story, the one who had asked the question conceded that he did indeed get the point. Jesus said to him, and vicariously to us: go out and do the same.

Persistence

Suppose you have a friend and you go to that person in the middle of the night. An unexpected visitor has arrived and there is nothing in your cupboard. You want to borrow food but your friend refuses, because it is the middle of the night. Be persistent. Bang on the door. You will be given whatever you need, not because of friendship, but because it is the middle of the night. (Lk 11:5–8)

⌒℮⌒

This parable in Luke follows the passage where Jesus teaches his disciples to pray: give us this day our daily bread. Persist in prayer. Never give up. A critically important lesson, but not the only one. There is the point about sharing, about meeting one another's needs, about going the extra mile when someone is clearly in a crisis. I am tempted to contest the story's conclusion. We do indeed go to a friend in an emergency. Isn't that what friends are for?

The one in charge

Who is the wise and faithful steward charged with seeing that all are fed at the appropriate time while the head of the house is away? Blessed is the one who is hard at work when the householder returns, for that person will be entrusted with overseeing all. But if the head of the house is delayed, and if the one in charge should be tempted to act abusively and to eat and drink licentiously, the one delayed may suddenly return. Then the insolent one would be caught by surprise and held accountable. (Mt 24:45–51)

This is another parable preparing us for the endtime. It warns us to be ready, for we know not the day nor the hour when we will be confronted with all we have said and done. It also says something about leadership, reminding us how we are to act when fulfilling a responsible role.

The rich fool

The land of one who was very rich produced an abundance of grain. In order to store such a bountiful harvest, barns were demolished and bigger ones built. The landowner was ecstatic, saying, eat! drink! be merry! These supplies will last for many years. Fool, said God, tonight you will die, and that is exactly what happened. All that wealth so selfishly hoarded, whose now will it be? (Lk 12:16–21)

Here is a parable of abundance. It seems like a legitimate surplus until one considers the underlying story implicit in the text. How did the landowner manage to acquire such extensive holdings? Who were the people who had worked the land and reaped that abundant harvest on somebody else's behalf? Were they peasants who went to bed hungry at night or lacked sufficient resources to provide a decent home for their families? In a world, then and now, where too few people have what they really need, the accumulation of inordinate wealth is an obscenity. When life here on earth is over, the things one has, whose will they be? It is appropriate that the parable ends on that evocative note. How do we see ourselves and our nation reflected in this story? What can we do to reestablish a balance of goods and services so that there is enough for all?

The rich and the poor

A person of privilege, fashionably dressed, ate lavishly every day. At the gate lay a poor soul covered with sores who longed to satisfy a perennial hunger with what fell from the rich person's table. The beggar died and was carried by angels to eternal bliss in heaven. The wealthy one also died and was sent to a place of torment. From the flames of Hades the tormented one looked up and saw the beggar — far, far away — and cried out, pleading for mercy. Please, dip the tip of your finger in water and touch my tongue with its coolness, for I am in agony! A heavenly voice recalled all the good things the tormented one had enjoyed and the evil the beggar had endured. Even now a chasm separated them, which no one could step across. Then send the beggar to warn my family, the one in agony pleaded, so that they might avoid this suffering. They have their leaders and prophets, the heavenly voice responded. They will not listen to them, came the cry of desperation, but they will repent when a warning

*comes from someone who has died. Alas, replied the voice
from heaven, if they ignore their leaders and prophets, they
will not pay attention to one who returns to them from the
dead. (Lk 16:19–31)*

⁓

This second parable on abundance highlights the juxtaposi-
tion of blatant excess and dire need. It reiterates the concern
of Jesus for those who are systemically poor, and it empha-
sizes the chasm separating those who will always have more
than enough from those who struggle to survive. While the
focus at first is on material things, it quickly shifts to another
dimension, where the one who once had everything is bereft
of what is essential, while the one who once had nothing,
suddenly has it all. We are reminded of those barns that were
filled to overflowing. The phrase "You can't take it with you"
keeps echoing in my ears.

Don't worry

*Don't worry about your life, what you will eat or how you
will clothe your body. For life is more than food and the body
far more than clothing. Consider that the birds neither sow
nor reap and have neither barn nor silo, and yet God feeds
them all. Can any of you by worrying add a single hour to
your span of life? If you cannot do something as small as this,
why worry about the rest? Consider the lilies of the field, how
they grow and how they flourish. They do not toil, nor do
they spin, yet Solomon in all his glory was never dressed like
one of these. If God so clothes the grass of the field, which*

is alive today but will be thrown in the oven tomorrow, how much more will God clothe you, O you of little faith! Do not be anxious about what to eat or what to drink, and above all, do not worry. The nations of the world require these things, and God knows, so do you. Seek first the reign of God, and all that you need will be given to you. (Lk 12:22–31)

‿✑‿

Keep calm. Don't worry. Easy for you to say. Well, no, it isn't easy. In a culture of acute anxiety, how can we keep on an even keel when so many things are beyond our control? Gone are those old securities, the promises made that all will be well. It seems like only yesterday that we thought we could manage a crisis. Our benefits were good, the savings were intact, the rent was fixed, our job was secure, we had seniority. But now, if catastrophe should strike or someone should happen to pull the plug, we would be less than a paycheck away from a shopping cart on the street. Oh yeah, sure, don't worry!

Dear Jesus, we simply cannot afford to lose faith in your promises, for that is our only surety when all else is in flux. The flowers of the field, the birds of the air, the babies in their bassinets, moms and dads in nursing homes, families of modest income with bills that just keep coming in, kids in the projects skeptical about getting an equal chance, those caught up in the violence of war, the violence of life, the throes of victimization, those who are ill, those who are dying — all turn expectantly to you, trusting and yes, believing, although please, forgive some disbelief, for doubt is so insidious. Please give us today our sustaining bread, and we will come back tomorrow. Please give us whatever we need to survive, and don't forget: bread *and* roses. Our hearts still ache for so much more than this world can provide. Those who seek for what will satisfy don't seem to know where to find it, but you know. Show us the way.

Memorize this powerful parable if it speaks to your heart as it spoke to mine. Make it your mantra for whenever you need a calming and a comforting word.

The wedding attendants

Ten of them took their lamps and went to meet the wedding party. Five were said to be foolish and five were said to be wise. Half had brought extra oil with them, but the other half had not. When the bride and bridegroom were delayed, all ten fell asleep. At midnight they were awakened. They are coming! Get up! Go out and meet them! They arose quickly and trimmed their lamps. Those who had brought no oil with them said to those who had extra flasks, give us some of your oil, for our lamps are going out. No, they replied, we may not have enough. Go out and buy some for yourselves. While they were away the ones who were ready led the wedding party into the banquet hall and the door was shut behind them. Later the others returned, pleading, open the door to us. Instead, they heard this chilling reply. Go away! I do not know who you are! (Mt 25:1–12)

                                         ∽

In Matthew, where this parable appears, ten women who are usually introduced as bridesmaids or as virgins, prepare to fulfill a traditional role. With lighted lamps they are to meet and accompany a wedding party to their destination. In the end, five of them do just that, while the others are rejected. We have heard this parable so many times from our teachers and our preachers that we can no longer hear the story apart from its interpretation and conventional application. It is about the endtime, about who will get into heaven, and why, and also who will not. Those who are foolishly unprepared and arrive at that decisive moment with no more oil in their lamps will not be admitted. Oil symbolically represents any or all of those virtues deserving of reward when our time on earth is over. Some things you can take with you, but none that can be shared. One has to earn eternal bliss solely on one's own. Indeed, there is some validity to this version of the story. However, I offer another perspective. If you want to see what I see, begin by asking some very pointed questions of the text.

We are set up at the start of the story to consider it a certain way. The women are grouped and already labeled. Five are foolish and five are wise. *Says who?* That is my first question. We are told that the so-called foolish take no oil with their lamps, while the so-called wise take flasks of oil, which suggests an ample supply. They are to carry lighted lamps, but some do not bring oil. *Why not?* All grow drowsy and fall asleep and awake at the appointed time. All ten women trim their lamps, but five are running low on oil, so they ask to borrow some. No! That was the word of the wise. *What kind of response is that?* Those with an ample supply of oil tell those who are running out of oil to go and buy some for themselves. *From whom?* The five depart. Those with oil join the wedding party and go with them into the banquet. The others return, but are not admitted. The host says from behind barred doors, I do not know who you are. *What kind of response is that?* Let us consider these questions, for a second storyline is emerging that we did not see before.

Wise and foolish. Good and bad. We know from the start just who will be the favored ones in this parable, so we follow the winning storyline right into heavenly bliss. Who among us would ever identify with someone said to be foolish? Which is precisely the problem with labels. If you don't like people, label them. Chances are, they will be shunned. The labels in this parable represent a specific perspective and an implicit interpretation written into the text.

We are told that the foolish brought no oil, which is not exactly accurate. When they awoke, they trimmed their lamps, which meant there was some oil in them. But the wedding party had been delayed, so the little they had would not be enough and their lamps were going out. The others had extra flasks of oil, but they refused to share them. A question of wise and foolish? Or a tale of have and have not enough? In a moment of crisis, those with a surplus chose to hoard their resources. They sent their colleagues on a wild goose chase, because where in the world would they get any oil in the middle of the night? Shops were shuttered at sundown. Family and friends were at home in bed. Remember the parable of the persistent friend? Imagine five frustrated women, banging on doors, calling for help, begging for oil in the middle of the night. The amazing thing is, they got it. Otherwise, they would not have returned. The so-called foolish were not so dumb, for they managed to get what they needed in order to survive.

Suddenly, we come to the end of the story, and we don't like what we see. The selfish sit at the banquet table, having sailed right into everlasting life beneath their shining lanterns. Those who labored for the little they had, who did nothing to deserve being relegated to the realm of eternal darkness, stand at the door and knock. Two gut-level questions remain to be asked. *Whose party is this anyway? Who is the one who barred the door?*

My inclination is to withhold an answer, for parables need to be wrestled with and their stories made our own. Let me frame my response this way. Traditionally we approach this story spiritually with a moral as its outcome. Oil and lamp become metaphors understood in a conventional way. Be sure not to fall short of love. Build up a supply of compassionate concern if you want to get to heaven. These images justify what would be a selfish, unloving action in any other context, for saying no to someone in need is not one of the virtues that will win you eternal life. From this point of view the wedding feast remains the heavenly banquet and Christ the perennial bridegroom who decides who can come in.

I imagine, however, the two-thirds world would approach this parable the other way, from the perspective of hard-core experience, where oil is really oil and there is never enough, where lamps that are lit too often go out, where the bar is set incredibly high, and even when the test is passed, access is still denied. This alternate understanding is based on a literal reading of the text, which in itself is ironic. It is just like Jesus to have written the dynamic of reversal into the storyline, hoping that people would get it, even though it might take a while. From a justice orientation, the foolish are wise and the wise foolishly follow the ways of the world right up to the very end, eating and drinking and making merry while the poor are kept outside. If this were the heavenly banquet, Jesus would never have barred the door, for whoever returns to him, is always — always — welcome.

Whatever you feel at this moment, go on to the final parable. It has an integral relationship to the story we have just heard and analyzed.

The least of these

Christ will come again in glory to separate the sheep from the goats, saying to those on the one side: inherit eternal bliss. For I was hungry and you gave me food, thirsty and you gave me something to drink, a stranger and you welcomed me, naked and you clothed me, sick and you took care of me, in prison and you visited me. Startled, the righteous will reply, when did we see you hungry and give you something to eat, or thirsty and give you something to drink? And when did we welcome you as a stranger or clothe you when you were naked? And when was it that we saw you sick or in prison and visited you? Then the Holy One will answer: what you did for the least of these, who are indeed my family, you did that for me. Then the one judging will say to the others: depart into eternal suffering. For I was hungry and you gave me no food, thirsty and you gave me nothing to drink, a stranger and you did not welcome me, naked and you did not clothe me, sick and in prison and you did not come. They too will be astonished and ask, when did we see you hungry or thirsty or a stranger or naked or sick or in prison and did

*not take care of you? And they will hear a similar reply: just
as you did not reach out to one of the least of these, my loved
ones, you did not reach out to me.* (Mt 25:31–46)

∽♾∾

This popular passage has taken on a life of its own. Many see
it as definitive of what it means to be Christian, its corporal
works of mercy a checklist against which we will be judged.
It is the third of three entries that make up chapter 25 of the
Gospel according to Matthew, and it functions as a lens for
interpreting the other two.

The parable of the wise and foolish women opens chapter 25. Our reinterpretation of the story of the lamps is
validated by this one's emphasis on "the least of these." Here
is another parable with an unexpected twist. The righteous
wonder where and when they could possibly have ministered
to Jesus. Those who failed the ultimate test are also caught
by surprise. Jesus gives examples. I was hungry and you gave
me food, thirsty and you gave me a drink. Tending to those
who are in need is prerequisite for reward. It seems obvious
in hindsight, but a lot less clear when face to face with reality
every day. The list is not conclusive. One suspects it might
go on and on. I was in prison and you failed to visit me. I was
in transition and you did not reach out to me. I had no oil to
light my lamp and you refused to share yours with me. This
third parable illuminates the story of the diminishing oil in
the flickering lamps and nudges it toward a this-worldly focus
with a more concrete application. One can imagine Jesus saying: whenever you were generous toward the least of these,
your gift was given to me.

~ 6 ~

Meals in the life of Jesus

At the heart of eucharist is the notion of putting ourselves once again in the presence of Jesus in the context of a meal. This sacramental association of Jesus present at a meal has historic precedence. Traditional Eucharist looks to the Last Supper as its primary source, while eucharist with a small "e" considers all the meals of Jesus, including that final supper. This wellspring of eucharistic theology and spirituality, long overshadowed in our emphasis on the final meal of Jesus, is the focus of this chapter. As we become familiar with these stories, as we tell them to one another, perhaps in the context of a meal, we will be led by the Spirit to know what to take and make our own, and we will experience how wisdom from the past can be transformative now.

✧

Prior to beginning his public ministry, Jesus is led by the Spirit of God into the Judean desert for a period of prayer and fasting. At the point when his hunger is extremely intense, he is strongly tempted to break his fast but is sustained by the realization that one does not live by bread alone. He did not disparage his physical needs but chose to acknowledge a higher power through an allegiance to God alone. At the end of his desert sojourn, angels came and waited on him, which probably means that his family and friends made a fabulous meal for him (Mt 4:1–11).

Sometime later in Samaria, when his disciples return after acquiring food, they find him engaged in conversation with one of the local women. Rabbi, eat something, they insist, but Jesus declines, saying that he has food to eat that they know nothing about. Horrified, for this is enemy territory, they say, surely no one else brought him food, for this would have violated their law. Jesus responds with words that encapsulate his calling. He said, my food is to do the will of the One who sent me and to complete God's work (Jn 4:31–34). To proclaim the compassionate reign of God, that is what feeds his spirit. Some hungers can be assuaged only by fidelity to one's purpose in life. On a very deep level, that is what sustains and nourishes.

Early in the Gospel according to John, we learn that Jesus performed his first miracle in the context of a meal.

A wedding in Cana

There was a wedding in Cana, a village in Galilee. The mother of Jesus was there. So were Jesus and his disciples. At the height of the festivities, Mary took Jesus aside, saying, there is no more wine. He seemed puzzled at her distress. Why tell him? It was not their concern. And it certainly wasn't the time or the place for him to get involved. His

mother simply told the servants to do as they were instructed.
Now six stone water jars used for purification rites were
standing nearby. Jesus said to the servants: fill the jars with
water. When they had done his bidding, he told them to draw
a sample for the chief steward's approval. When the steward
had tasted the new wine, he wondered where it had come
from, although the servants knew. He called the bridegroom
and congratulated him, saying, everyone serves the good wine
first and then inferior wine, when their guests are less likely
to notice. But you have kept the best until last. (Jn 2:1–11)

⟞⟞⟞⟋⟋

This was the first of many signs associated with Jesus. What
he did in Cana to appease his mother invested a village wedding with lasting significance. The question that immediately
comes to mind is, whose wedding was it anyway? Why was
Mary so concerned? Why did Jesus get involved when he
clearly did not want to? It must have been a family wedding,
for Mary and her son played prominent roles. Most likely the
bride was Mary's niece, the daughter of her sister, the sister
who, years later, would stand beside her at the foot of the
cross, as John's Gospel records (19:25), and was constantly
with him, together with his mother and Mary Magdalene, as
the Gnostic *Gospel of Philip* reports. No wonder Mary was
agitated and urged her son to do something. She may have
suggested he take the servants and go borrow some wine from
the neighbors. As first cousin and as eldest son, Jesus would
have been responsible for doing everything within his power
to restore tranquility to his family circle at this most sensitive

time. And indeed, he did. His actions that day added another dimension to his presence among them. Ironically, when they saw the results, they could not believe it was real.

Peter's mother-in-law

They had just left the synagogue — Peter, Andrew, James, and John in the company of Jesus — and were on their way to Peter's house, most likely for a meal. Peter's mother-in-law was in bed suffering from a fever. When Jesus took her by the hand, the fever left her instantly, and she got up and served them. (Lk 4:38–39)

⌐℮⌐

What was the point of preserving this memory of Peter's mother-in-law? It really isn't news when a woman puts a meal on the table, even if she is sick. Yet all three Synoptic writers record the incident, so it must have made an impact. What we know is that she was cured of a fever and that she got up and served them. How did she serve? The word used here that indicates "to serve" also means "to minister." Had Peter's mother-in-law been distraught because her son-in-law had left home to follow an itinerant preacher? Was her daughter also about to join the circle of female disciples? Was all that resolved when Jesus arrived with Peter to share a meal? Did Jesus take her by the hand and say to her, "Come, follow me"? Did she minister to their immediate needs and then later on join the Galilean women who ministered to and with Jesus? These are distinct possibilities.

Dinner in Matthew's house

One day as Jesus was walking along, he saw a man named Matthew sitting at a tax booth and said to him: follow me. He got up and followed him. Later that evening Jesus was a guest at dinner in Matthew's house. Sitting at table and eating with him were many tax collectors and sinners, as well as others who had followed him. The Pharisees were scandalized. Why? they asked his disciples. Why would their teacher choose to eat with tax collectors and sinners? Jesus overheard them. It is not those who are well but those who are sick who need a physician, he said. I have come to call not the righteous, but those who are sinners.

(Mt 9:9–13)

∽

One thing is clear from this narrative. Jesus stood in direct opposition to the restrictive regulations imposed by religious authority, and he did so publicly. He not only called an outcast to come and follow him, but he also went to eat with him and with his associates, who were also stigmatized. Jesus sought out the company of those who had been segregated by society and designated as sinners and was prepared to accept the consequences for the principles he upheld. Who in this story needs healing? Who was Jesus referring to when he pointed out that the sick were the ones in need of a physician? What systemic illnesses need to be cauterized and healed?

Feeding five thousand

After an exhausting period, Jesus withdrew to a deserted place, but the crowds followed him there. They came on foot from surrounding towns, a vast number of people, including families with children. Jesus was moved to compassion and cured the sick among them. Hours passed. It was getting late, and the disciples were growing more concerned because it would soon be dark. Then what would all those people do in such an isolated place? The disciples would have dismissed the crowd so they could go into the village for food, but Jesus would not let them. He told them not to send them away, but to give them something to eat. His disciples were incredulous. They had only five loaves and two fish. What was that among so many? Jesus told everyone to sit on the ground. He gave thanks and said a blessing. Then he broke the bread and divided the fish and gave what he had to his disciples to distribute to the crowd. All of them ate and were satisfied. They collected the leftover pieces of bread, filling twelve baskets. The estimate of how many had been served was five thousand men, plus many more women and children.

(Mt 14:13–21)

✧

Eucharistic images shape this narrative, adding a layer of interpretation to the telling of the story. Metaphors abound that call to mind the suffering of so many people who are impoverished and oppressed. An isolated place. Running out of time. Hordes of sick and hungry folk lacking what is needed to feed them. Then suddenly, there is more than enough. Now where did that all come from? They say there is enough food to go around, but enough food just doesn't get around. It is hoarded in isolated places. Sharing starts a chain reaction. Such sharing is sacramental. The little we have might seem too little, but keep on adding a little bit more until there is enough. The narrative is focused on physical food, on satisfying hunger. That was a priority for Jesus. It is a priority now. Jesus invited everyone to sit down and share a meal together. That in itself was a miracle.

Both Matthew and Mark also record the feeding of four thousand (Mt 15:32–39), which may have been a separate event or simply a separate tradition that evolved from a singular source. Because that account is similar in many ways to the narrative above, it has not been included here.

The lesson of the bread

When they reached the other side of the lake, the disciples discovered they had forgotten to bring bread. Jesus warned them to be wary of the yeast of the Pharisees and Sadducees. What in the world was he talking about? Were they being chastised for forgetting the bread? When Jesus realized they had misunderstood, he said to them: you of little faith, why are you talking about having no bread? Do you still not get it? Have you already forgotten that five loaves fed five thousand men and a lot of women and children, with how many baskets left over? How could you fail to understand? I am not speaking about bread. I say to you again, be wary of the yeast of the Pharisees and Sadducees. Then they realized that yeast did not mean bread but the teachings of the Pharisees and Sadducees. (Mt 16:5–12)

⁓

This meal story is about a missed meal and about reflecting on a meal that is already past in order to learn a lesson from it. Jesus often spoke in images and metaphors, so that even when they had experienced the practical application of what he had been saying, the disciples did not always get it. They are told to be wary of the teaching of certain authority figures within institutional religion. He wants them to think more critically about the incident of the loaves and fish. For example, a number of people who shared that meal should not have been eating together, according to the law. They were not only given something to eat, but given permission to eat together. Jesus may have been reminding them of that. What does this story remind us of or prod us to reconsider? We are much too enamored with what is literal and concrete, thereby missing the messages that metaphors convey.

Bread of life

Jesus had gone off by himself again. That day he was on the other side of the sea, and still the disciples found him. Why had he come there, they wanted to know, but he never really answered. Instead, he returned to the theme of food, saying: do not settle for food that perishes; seek food that endures for eternal life. He spoke of the bread from heaven that gives life to the world. Give us bread such as this, they pleaded, remembering the loaves. Jesus said: I am the bread of life.

Whoever comes to me will never hunger; whoever believes in me will never thirst. They began to whisper among themselves because he claimed to be bread from heaven. Some said they knew who his father was and others had met his mother. Was he not Jesus, son of Joseph? How could he say that he came from heaven? Jesus interrupted them and told them to stop bickering among themselves. Holding firm to his word, he repeated: whoever believes has eternal life. I am the bread of life. (Jn 6:25–48)

⁓

This significant passage witnesses to the humanity of Jesus in the midst of mystical claims. He is Jesus, Mary's son. His father's name is Joseph. He hails from the village of Nazareth. All the locals know him. Yet he says he came to earth from heaven. Well, now, didn't we all? He says he is the bread of life. What did he mean by that? A significant portion of the scripture text that offers an explanation has been omitted in this retelling. Its sacramental language reflects the influence of a later time, outlining a eucharistic theology and practice that belong to the developing church. Nevertheless, the power of the metaphor linking Jesus and bread with everlasting life evokes an association with eucharist that is authentic to the core. This story gives witness to Jesus as eucharist with a small "e" for it is his Spirit that nourishes us in the fullness of our humanity, revealing to us an integration of both human and divine.

A woman in the crowd

*A woman in the crowd surrounding Jesus cried out to him
with a loud voice. Blessed is the womb that bore you! Blessed
are the breasts that nursed you! Jesus responded. Blessed are
those who hear and obey the word of God! (Lk 11:27–28)*

❧

An anonymous woman blesses the mother who gave birth to
Jesus, and she blesses the breasts that fed him. Mary was the
source of this holy man's first most formative meals. For nine
months her placenta provided all the nourishment needed for
the developing fetus. After her child was delivered, for twice
nine months and then some, Mary's breast milk nurtured and
satisfied her developing baby. No one but his mother was
with him at the welcome table during those first meals. Jesus
drank in her spirit and embraced her hospitality, and then
replenished them in her. How often do we remember and
give thanks for those prenatal meals from our mothers and
our nurturing after birth? But wait, the woman's blessing appears to be contradicted by Jesus. Another tug of war between
word and sacrament? Not necessarily. Think of his response
as, Yes...but...and not as either/or. After the initial tending, the one who has given birth to an independent life form
must also continue to grow and develop in wisdom and in
grace and in the liberating word of God. To hear and obey the
word of God means sometimes one has to close one's ears to
contravening voices, even from authoritative sources. This is
particularly true for women. Mary had to do so. The women

witnesses of the resurrection certainly had to do so. They heard the word of the Spirit speak, and they chose to obey.

⎯⎯⎯

At the home of Jairus

A leader of the synagogue approached Jesus in the midst of a crowd of people. He fell at his feet and begged him to come heal his only daughter who was dying and who was only twelve years old. Before Jesus could follow Jairus home, the crowd enveloped him, and a woman who had bled for twelve years and could find no one to cure her made her way to Jesus. She touched the hem of his garment, and immediately, the bleeding stopped. Who touched me? Jesus wanted to know, for he had felt power go out from him. Trembling, the woman came forward and told why she had touched him and how she had been healed. He praised her faith, which had led to her healing, and told her to go in peace. By this time word had arrived from Jairus. His little girl had died. Jesus went to their house anyway and was met by weeping and wailing. He told the mourners not to weep, that she was only sleeping, but they knew that she had died. Joined by her father and mother, and by Peter and James and John, he entered her bedroom, took her hand, and told her to get up. She got up at once. Her parents were jubilant and everyone was astounded. In the midst of their joyous celebration, Jesus told her parents to be sure to give her something to eat. (Lk 8:40–56)

⎯⎯⎯

Two miracle stories intertwine, the story of a woman who has bled for twelve years and the story of a dying twelve-year-old girl. Jesus is interrupted as he is about to follow Jairus home to heal his dying daughter, and the young girl's life is interrupted as Jesus is caught up in another's need. The delay heightens the suspense and raises the stakes for the miracle worker, for the need now goes beyond healing to giving life back to the dead. The woman, lifted from the depths of despair, is given a whole new lease on life. The little girl, raised up from the dead, is restored to life in anticipation of all that is yet to be. Can you imagine the festive celebration as her parents took her into their arms? Food arriving from everywhere, the finest dishes of family and friends, the favorite treats of a little lost girl who has found her way into a future, and Jesus in the midst of all this chaos as their honored and reverenced guest. Scripture does not mention a meal. It records the cryptic phrase from Jesus: *give her something to eat.* Not as a proof of resurrection here, but simply a reassuring word that their precious child is safely home and life can get back to normal. Did you ever feel that all was lost only to experience what can only be called a miraculous turn of events? Death to life is a process of life that is going on all around us. We need only to count the ways.

At the home of Zaccheus

As Jesus was passing through Jericho, a rich tax collector named Zaccheus tried to catch a glimpse of him but was unable to do so, because he was short in stature and the crowds got in the way. So he ran and climbed a sycamore

tree along the route where Jesus would pass. When Jesus
looked up and saw Zaccheus, he told him to hurry on down,
for he wanted to spend the day at his house. Zaccheus was
delighted to welcome him, but many in the crowd began to
object, for he would be the guest of a sinner. Zaccheus began
to defend himself, telling how he would share his earnings,
giving half of what he possessed to the poor and repaying
fourfold anyone to whom anything was owed. For this Jesus
praised Zaccheus, telling him that this very day salvation
would come to his house. (Lk 19:1–10)

☙

Here is another story where a meal is not explicitly mentioned
but it happened nonetheless. Jesus had been on the road. Hot,
thirsty, jostled by the crowds, he is more than ready to take a
break and he opts to spend the whole day at the house of the
wealthy Zaccheus. There is more than one meal implicit here.
Lunch, snacks, drinks, dinner. Food would have been abundant, succulent, and sumptuous. From what we know from
the Gospel accounts, Jesus did fast on occasion, but he seems
to have been more oriented to feasts and festivity. Here the
meal does not take center stage, putting the spotlight rather
on such values as ingenuity, hospitality, generosity, determi-
nation, and conversion, to mention just a few. To which of
these do you relate at this particular time?

A place at the table

Jesus said this to his disciples. Who among you would say
to your servant who has just come in from plowing or from

tending sheep in the field, Come, take your place at the table. *Would you not rather say,* Prepare my supper for me. Put on your apron and serve me while I eat and drink. You may eat your own meal later. *Then do you thank your servant for doing what you have commanded? So also, when you have done all that you have been ordered to do, say,* We are worthless servants, for we have done only what we ought to have done! *(Lk 17:7–10)*

❦

There is a tad of irony here and a generous dose of truth telling. The one who would later put on an apron and wash the feet of his disciples wants his followers to think about changing their own segregated ways. He knows exactly what they would do, and he goads them into considering how they really ought to behave. Everyone has a place at his table. It is time for them to turn the tables on societal expectations that dominate and exclude. Once we overcome our tendency to take scripture literally, we will discover much in this story that is applicable to us.

On the sabbath

Jesus and his disciples were walking through the grain fields. This happened on the sabbath. His disciples, who were hungry, began to eat the heads of grain as they were walking along. The Pharisees confronted Jesus. His disciples were breaking the sabbath law. Jesus reminded them of a precedent in their own tradition. David and his companions, when they were hungry and had no food, entered the house of God

and ate the bread of the Presence, which is reserved only
for priests. Then Jesus said, in his own words, that the sabbath was made for humankind, and not humankind for the
sabbath. (Mk 2:23–28)

ᴄᴇ᷈ᴏ

The Pharisees were often opposed to Jesus, not only because
he broke the law, but because he reinterpreted tradition. Jesus
did not espouse a flagrant disregard for law, but took every
opportunity to say that there are times when human need
overrides the law, when one must answer to a higher law,
when an inner authority indicates that a particular regulation
does not apply.

Eating with unwashed hands

*Pharisees and scribes who had come from Jerusalem gath-
ered around Jesus. They noticed that some of his disciples
were eating with unwashed hands, so they asked him why
the tradition of the elders was not given due respect. Citing
the prophet Isaiah, Jesus rebuked the Pharisees and scribes
for being hypocritical, honoring God with their lips while
dishonoring God in their hearts. To indoctrinate with human
precepts is to worship God in vain. They had rejected God's
commandment in favor of their own tradition. He concluded:
what comes out of a person defiles that person and not what
is taken in. Evil intentions that come from the heart defile
one from within. (Mt 15:1–20)*

ᴄᴇ᷈ᴏ

Here is another incident where Jesus challenged religious authority. Their legislation had taken precedence again over the more flexible law of love, revealing the chasm that separated their ways from his own. He refused to tolerate hypocrisy and was not afraid to say so. Exchanges such as this one often took place at a meal.

Dinner with a leader of the Pharisees

Jesus went to the house of a leader of the Pharisees to eat a meal on the sabbath. They were watching him very closely, to catch him if he should step out of line. Suddenly, a man afflicted with dropsy came and stood in front of him. Turning to the lawyers and Pharisees, Jesus asked them if it was lawful or not lawful to cure people on the sabbath. He waited for an answer. Hearing none, he healed the man. Then he sent him home. In the ensuing silence, he challenged those who had witnessed this violation of the sabbath, saying, what if your child or your ox fell into a well on the sabbath? Wouldn't you rescue it immediately, even though it is the sabbath? No one replied. (Lk 14:1–6)

∽

There he goes again, throwing down the gauntlet by curing a man on the sabbath in front of those responsible for upholding the law. What else was he to do? Core to his teaching was the conviction that the sabbath was made for people and not the other way around. Here was a man with a physical ailment that was quite debilitating, standing there looking him in the eye. Jesus, moved to compassion, had no other choice but to heal him. He challenged his leaders to prove him wrong, but for some reason, they did not.

At the house of a Pharisee

Jesus accepted an invitation to dinner at a Pharisee's house. He took his place at table without washing before he ate. Knowing his host would not be pleased, he was the first to speak of it and did not mince his words. Addressing the Pharisees sharply, he accused them of cleaning the outside of the cup and ignoring the wickedness within. He reminded them: the one who made the outside of the cup also made the inside. He challenged them to tithe what was within and be cleansed both inside and out. Woe to you Pharisees, he declared, for tithing all kinds of external things and neglecting justice and the love of God. These are what should have been practiced. Woe to you Pharisees, he said again, for craving the synagogue's seat of honor and for wanting to be greeted with respect when in the marketplace. He then compared them to unmarked graves that people walk on unaware of what is lying beneath them. (Lk 11:37–44)

༺༻

An instinctive response would be to say that Jesus will not be invited back there for dinner anytime soon. Which leads one to question why Jesus ate so many meals with Pharisees. There is no easy answer. Perhaps it was because not all of them were his enemies, and some may have been his friends. Because they had a heritage in common and could handle the give and take. Because Jesus was a curiosity to them and they were a challenge to him. Because they had something to say to each other, conflicting visions and ideologies and a flair for wrestling with issues, which would make dinner conversation anything but dull. Jesus disagreed strongly with their system and its application, as this narrative clearly shows, but this was his faith tradition too, and his intent was to reform it. He spoke of his vision and his views whenever the occasion presented itself. Even in social settings, he was quick to speak his mind. He was on a mission to soften the stranglehold of religion and the burdens it imposed. Therefore, he took every opportunity to challenge the ruling class so that those charged with keeping the law and with safeguarding tradition did not become a law unto themselves. Eventually, his words and deeds would be used against him when be was brought to trial.

A woman anoints his feet

Jesus was invited to dinner by one of the Pharisees. When he had entered Simon's house and had taken his place at table, a woman, said to be a sinner, cautiously approached him with an alabaster jar. She knelt at his feet, weeping, and began to bathe his feet with her tears and dry them with her hair. She kissed his feet again and again and anointed them with ointment. The Pharisee saw this and said to himself, surely, if this man were a prophet, he would know what sort of woman is touching him; he would know she is a sinner. As if he had read his thoughts, Jesus turned to Simon and said the following words to him: A creditor had two debtors. One owed him five hundred denarii, the other owed him fifty. Since neither of them could pay him, he canceled the debts for both. Now which one loves him more? Simon replied, it was probably the one for whom the greater debt was forgiven. Jesus agreed, and then made his point. Do you see this woman? he asked. I came to your house as your dinner guest, but you gave me no water to wash my feet, while this woman has bathed my feet with her tears and dried them with her hair. You gave me no welcoming kiss, nor did you anoint my head with oil, yet she has covered my feet with kisses and anointed them with ointment. Therefore, I tell you, her sins, though many, have all been forgiven, because she has shown great love. The one to whom little is forgiven shows only a little love. Then Jesus reassured the woman that her sins were indeed forgiven. Those who were with him at table began to whisper among themselves, saying, who does he think he is? Who is he to forgive sins? Jesus turned to the woman and told her it was her faith that had saved her, and that she could go now in peace. (Lk 7:36–50)

∽℘∾

This story of love and forgiveness speaks to the heart of the mission of Jesus. It certainly had people talking. A woman judged by others pours out her pain at the feet of Jesus and leaves to face the future with her head held high. The woman in the following narrative, which tells of another meal at another time with a different cast of characters, has been confused at times with the woman described above.

Dinner at Bethany

Several days before the Passover, Jesus came to Bethany, to the home of Martha and Mary and their brother Lazarus. The dinner was in thanksgiving for Lazarus, whom Jesus had raised from the dead. Lazarus was given a place of honor at the table with Jesus and their other guests. While Martha was serving the meal, Mary appeared with a generous amount of very expensive perfume. She anointed the feet of Jesus, then wiped them with her hair, and the house was filled with the fragrance. Judas Iscariot condemned the waste, but he was quickly silenced by Jesus, who told him to leave her alone.

(Jn 12:1–8)

Jesus was often in Bethany at the family home of his beloved friends, Mary and Martha and Lazarus. This dinner was a very special celebration in honor of Lazarus, who recently had come back from the dead. His sisters figure prominently in yet another narrative in which they have similar roles. What exactly are those roles? There is so much more behind the story than can be dealt with here. Be sure to share your own thoughts about it, and tell it over and over again.

A meal with Martha and Mary

Martha, joined by her sister, Mary, welcomed Jesus when he visited her home. Mary sat at his feet listening attentively to all that he had to say, while Martha kept doing what had to be done to put a meal on the table. Distracted by her many tasks, she complained to Jesus about being left to do all the work alone and asked him to tell her sister to give her a helping hand. Martha, Martha, was his reply, you are worried about so many things when only one thing is needed. Mary has chosen the better part and it will not be taken from her. (Lk 10:38–42)

A woman anoints his head

Jesus was in Bethany at the house of Simon the leper. He was sitting at the table when a woman with an alabaster jar of very costly ointment broke open the jar and poured the precious ointment on his head. Some were angry at this waste. They felt the ointment could have been sold and the income given to the poor. They continued to criticize her until Jesus told them to let her alone. He approved of what she had done for him. The poor, he said, will always be with you. I, on the other hand, will not. She anointed my body in preparation for all that is to come. Wherever in the world the good news is proclaimed, what she has done will be told to others in memory of her. (Mk 14:3–9)

꿍

Imagine the response to hearing that Jesus ate a meal at the house of a leper. The stigma of leprosy was so deeply entrenched that those afflicted were lifelong social and religious outcasts. To associate with them was forbidden, to share a meal unthinkable. That in itself would have been the subject of conversations far and wide. The focal point of the narrative, however, is really an anointing. An extravagant anointing.

By a woman whose predicted notoriety remains shrouded in anonymity. She may have been one of the women disciples, for her presence is not an issue, but the use of her property is. Some at the dinner seemed to think they had a stake in what belonged to her and loudly bemoaned the windfall that had just been thrown away. If Judas were present at this meal, and there is no reason to think that he wasn't, he would have been one of the voices raised against wasting such a lucrative resource on anointing the body of Jesus, just as he did at Bethany. Hours later he would deliver the body of Jesus to a crucifying death for a very paltry sum. Jesus had intended that the woman's story be told in memory of her to commemorate her prophetic action. Yet at every Eucharist we remember instead Judas and his act of ultimate betrayal when we introduce the words of institution with this despicable phrase: "On the night he was betrayed. . . . "

The Last Supper

On the first day of Unleavened Bread, when the Passover lamb is sacrificed, the disciples asked where they should go to prepare the Passover meal. Jesus sent two of them into the city to ask the owner of a house to show them the large room upstairs that had been set aside for their use. They went and found it as he had said and began to make preparations. When it was evening and all was ready, Jesus arrived with his disciples and they took their place at table. During the meal Jesus revealed that one of them would betray him. Those sitting near him were distressed. One by one they asked him quietly, are you referring to me? He said it was someone eating with him, dipping bread into the bowl with him. Then Judas Iscariot turned to Jesus and brazenly asked, is it I? You know the answer, Jesus replied. While they were eating, Jesus took a loaf of bread, blessed it, broke it, and gave it to them, saying, "This is my body." *Then he took a cup, gave thanks, and said,* "This is my blood of the covenant, which is poured out for many." *He would not drink wine again, he said, until the reign of God is fully realized. (Mk 14:12–25)*

⸎

Was this a Passover meal? The Synoptic writers say it was. According to John, it was not. He explicitly states in his Gospel that the crucifixion took place on the day of preparation, which would mean that the death of Jesus coincided with the ritual slaughter of the Passover lambs, a theological association at the heart of Eucharist. The discrepancy regarding dates and therefore the fundamental nature of the meal has never been reconciled.

What about the women? Those women who formed the Galilean circle of female disciples, and Mary the mother of Jesus. They had come to Jerusalem for the festival and remained to stand at the foot of the cross and keep vigil at the tomb. They were the first eyewitnesses to confirm that Jesus rose from the dead. Where did they eat their Passover meal if not together with Jesus? The room was large, the text records, suggesting that more than thirteen men would be coming to the table. Disciples asked where the meal would be so they could begin preparations. Who would have posed such a practical question and then done something about it? With the sense of imminent danger that seemed to touch them all, wouldn't the family of Jesus and his community of disciples, which included women and men, want to stay together, want to be with Jesus at such an important festival time? When Jesus arrived that evening with those of his inner circle, everything was ready. Common sense says, and the text allows, that others — women and children — were already there.

What transpired that evening? Far more than we can tell. A confluence of contradictory moods and a feeling of urgency made this meal like no other. Passover memories and metaphors provided a subtext ripe with significance. From now on the traditional blessing of bread before a festive meal, perhaps before every ordinary meal, would never be the same. Whatever words were said by Jesus, one thing is certain: he invested a familiar ritual with an unforgettable meaning. The memory of the moment continues to live on.

From John's account of that evening, we learn of a foot-washing ritual that the other evangelists did not record.

෬ᆺᄼ

During supper Jesus got up from the table, took off his outer garment, and fastened a towel around his waist. He poured water into a basin and began to wash the feet of his disciples and to dry them with the towel. Peter was indignant and refused to let Jesus wash his feet. Jesus explained to him that although he was confused at the moment, later he would understand. Never, said Peter forcefully; he would never let Jesus wash his feet. Unless he was allowed to do so, Peter would no longer be a part of him. Those words got through to Peter. He told Jesus to wash, not only his feet, but also his hands and his head! Jesus said it would not be necessary, for those who have bathed are clean and need only to wash their feet. Then he said, you are clean, but not all of you, for he knew who would betray him. After he had washed their feet and put on his robe, he returned to his place at the table and explained to them what he had done. You call me your teacher and leader, he said, and you are right, because I am. So if I have washed your feet, then you ought to wash one another's feet. I have set you an example. Do to one another as I have done to you. (Jn 13:1–15)

᳉᳉

In John's account Jesus leaves his place at the table to perform a menial service. He washes the feet of those who are sharing the meal with him. This reversal of custom and expectation turns things upside down. It is his teaching moment. He explains that what he has done may make no sense to them now, but one day they will understand. Meanwhile, they are to do as he has done, tend to the needs of one another by ministering to each other. It is an egalitarian gesture, for the one who has rank and authority has identified with the least among them. He has shown that genuine leadership is expressed in service, which does not mean servitude. This symbolic action has a prominent place within Christian tradition, even though foot washing is not part of the culture of our Western world.

For the next four chapters the evangelist records what he recalls of the final discourse of Jesus and his concluding prayer on that memorable night. This is one of our richest resources, giving a certain texture and tenderness to Jesus. It resurrects the Jesus that speaks to our heart. It doesn't really matter if someday we discover that some of the words John attributes

to Jesus really belong to John, for the truth within the discourse transcends its literary limitations. It is surprising that
the words of institution are not included in John's account.
This may be because by the time of this Gospel it was danger-
ous to be openly Christian. By then their rites were held in
secret and the sacred texts protected. Some think that the foot
washing ritual was John's symbolic substitute for the words of
institution. Or those words may be encoded in his passage on
the eucharist in chapter 6, verses 52–58.

~ 7 ~

Resurrection meals

It was early on the first day of the week, and there was chaos among the disciples of Jesus. The women who had gone to the tomb with spices in order to anoint his broken body had found the stone removed and were saying that the tomb was empty. They had seen some sort of apparition. Jesus was alive. Mary Magdalene had certainly seen him and had even spoken with him. The women knew from experience that Jesus had risen from the dead, but the men did not believe them. Here and there he began appearing to the disciples at a meal, doing what he did before he died, proclaiming a liberating word, projecting a presence that more than filled the physical space he occupied. It was said that he appeared to those "who were chosen by God as witnesses, and who ate and drank with him after he rose from the dead" (Acts 10:41). The resurrection meals of Jesus bridge the gap between what had been and the new understanding that was to come. Transition from flesh to spirit would not be an easy journey for any of them, but it was the road they had to travel, alone and, at times, together.

Emmaus

Later that day, two of the disciples were returning to Emmaus, a village within walking distance of Jerusalem. They were engaged in a spirited exchange, reliving all the events of that week, when a stranger came up beside them and joined in their conversation. He seemed to know very little of what had recently transpired, so they filled him in on the details. Jesus, a prophet, had been crucified, but his body was no longer in the tomb. Women disciples had a vision of angels who said he was alive. Some men saw the empty tomb, but they did not see Jesus.

When they paused, Jesus admonished them for being foolish and slow of heart to believe the witness of the prophets. Then he walked them through the scriptures as he walked along with them, integrating his own story as he interpreted the texts. They listened to him, mesmerized, not knowing who he was.

As they approached their village, they pressed him to stay the night with them, for it was already evening and the light was almost gone. As they sat at the table together, about to share a meal, Jesus took and blessed the bread, broke it, and shared it with them. Suddenly their eyes were opened, and in an instant he was gone. In the flush of recognition, they felt their hearts burning as they recalled the words he had spoken to them during their journey home.

They set out at once along that same road back to Jerusalem. There they found the disciples gathered in a spirit of jubilation. They were saying that Jesus had risen. The two from Emmaus told their story of what happened on the road and how they had known it was Jesus in the breaking of the bread at home. (Lk 24:13–35)

⤞⤝

Where exactly was Emmaus? No one knows for certain. Seven miles from Jerusalem, if we are to take Luke literally, although an ancient Palestinian tradition maintains it was a village once named Amwas twenty miles away. That would mean quite a walk for the two disciples, twice twenty miles in a single day, but it certainly could be done. Emmaus means "warm wells" in Hebrew. There were two warm wells at Amwas.

A more pressing question persists. Who were the two disciples? One is said to be Cleopas. The other is unidentified. Since the Greek phrase for "two of them" is not gender specific, I am convinced one of them was a woman, the wife of Cleopas, and that husband and wife were discussing what had happened in Jerusalem as they were returning home. If we listen to their conversation, we will hear hints of "he said, she said" in the dialogue. The women saw a vision of angels. The men saw an empty tomb. The women said he was alive. The men did not believe them. Surely the one who tenaciously supported the women's perspective must have been there among them, a member of their circle. While husband and wife were conversing, Jesus joined them and eventually interjected: "How foolish you are and slow to believe the witness of the prophets!" The conversation continued as Jesus reviewed and reinterpreted scripture. Was he validating women's prophetic witness with proof texts from the scripture? Whatever it was they were talking about, it remained an intellectual exercise until they sat down together to partake of a meal.

If we are still not convinced that one of the two disciples was a woman, consider the anecdotal evidence at the end of the day. When they arrived in Emmaus, they invited Jesus into their home. Clearly, this was a couple offering hospitality to a guest who gratefully accepted their offer of both lodging and a meal. Then something Jesus said or did — a look, a gesture, a unique way of expressing his *berakah* before eating — was instantly recognized. When Jesus knew they knew, not only who he was but what his appearance among them was all about, his mission was accomplished, and suddenly he was gone.

The couple returned to Jerusalem. It did not matter how late it was or how long the way that lay ahead, for their hearts burned within them. They were on a road already taken, retracing their steps, embracing the journey, seeing it and understanding it now as they never had before. Once our eyes are opened, we can no longer remain in place. We may resist convincing. Jesus tried hard to show how everything had changed, whether or not one could see it, but they, as we, don't always get it. Once we see what we had failed to see, once we change perspective, we simply must move on. They returned to where they had started from and nothing was the same. Some who had been dismissive before now passionately believed. The two from Emmaus testified that their own eyes had been opened and they had come to know Jesus at the breaking of the bread.

Let us return to Emmaus for a moment and look a little closer at the breaking of the bread. This action of Jesus has long been considered a prototype of the Eucharist. If a woman recognized Jesus as he broke bread for the first time after that last time with his disciples when something unforgettable had taken place at his final meal, would that not suggest that at least one woman had been present at the Last Supper? One wonders how Eucharist would have evolved if this were the story and the interpretation that had been handed on. Is that why the wife of Cleopas has been eliminated from the text? For I believe she was. John in his Gospel identifies Mary, wife of Clopas, as one of the four women who stood at the foot of the cross (19:25). It is logical to conclude that Mary, wife of Clopas, was the wife of Cleopas, even though the spelling of her name differs slightly from that of her husband and there are lengthy arguments to insist it was otherwise. All it took from a scribe was to eliminate a single letter from her name, intentionally or inadvertently, and she is written out of history, one less female eyewitness to testify to the facts. Neither Mary of Clopas nor Cleopas is mentioned anywhere else in the Gospel texts.

A final word about that Emmaus meal. Something equally significant may have been lost in the swirl of eucharistic assumptions, namely, the very nature of the meal. Having spent time in a significant number of villages around the world, I find it hard to imagine that the couple returned home to an empty house, as depictions of the Emmaus meal suggest. Where was the rest of the family, and their extended family, and where in the world were the neighbors? In a village where the usual layout consists of closely connected compounds and a whole lot of curious people, one would expect a raucous welcome no matter what time of day or night. Here was news from the city. Break out the wine, bring loaves and olives, help put some things on the table. Surely that is where the food came from — family members, neighbors, and friends — for no one is going to whip up a meal having just walked home from Jerusalem. To break bread meant to share a meal. Picture a small mob milling around, eating, drinking, heatedly discussing the week's tragic events and their unanticipated outcome. Then in all that chaos the couple suddenly realizes the stranger is gone. In a flash they comprehend. He was here. With us. We felt his spirit. Jesus was here in the midst of us, and his spirit will continue to live on in us. Here is eucharist with a small "e," proclaiming a continuity between those meals in the life of the historical Jesus and the meals where the spirit of Jesus mingles among and within his followers through all the years to come. There is so much in this story that resonates with us.

The upper room

While they were talking about all of this, suddenly, there was Jesus, standing in the midst of them. Peace be with you, he said to them. They were startled, and some were terrified, for they thought they were seeing a ghost. Jesus asked them why they were frightened and why there were so many doubts in their hearts. He showed them his hands and his feet and said that a ghost does not have flesh and bones. Look. Come close. Touch me, he said. They were tentative, hesitant, as they wondered how they ought to respond, when Jesus asked them for something to eat. They gave him a piece of broiled fish, and he ate it in right there in front of them. Then he

spoke to them, opening their minds, until their joy completely
overshadowed the depth of their disbelief. You are witnesses
of these things, he said. Then he charged them to stay right
where they were until they were empowered from on high.

(Lk 24:36–49)

⁓

This is a curious passage. The disciples were together in Jerusalem at the end of a very long day. The two from Emmaus
had arrived exhausted in the middle of the night and had
witnessed enthusiastically to their encounter with Jesus. All
in the room knew firsthand, or else they knew from hearsay,
that Jesus had risen from the dead. Then why, when he appeared to them, did they still not believe it? Why did they
doubt? Why were they afraid? The most logical answer is,
because not all of them had seen him. Yes, there were eyewitnesses in the group, but except for Cleopas from Emmaus,
those eyewitnesses were women. Perhaps their testimony had
swayed a few, but many still felt these were fanciful tales, and
they did not believe them. It was going to take more than a
woman's word to bring some men around. So Jesus appeared
in the midst of the Jerusalem disciples to let them see him
for themselves. Again, there are eucharistic overtones to the
appearance of Jesus. Was this the same room in which they
had met the night before he died? Were they sitting at table
when Jesus asked them to give him something to eat? Did
they share a meal with him and not simply hand him a piece
of fish? It is highly unlikely he ate alone to prove he was not
an apparition.

This is a story about real presence, the real presence of the risen Jesus to the devastated community. There he was to corroborate the testimony of those eyewitnesses among them. He will do the same for us when we are called to testify to what we have seen and heard. The experience of Jesus really present with his disciples at a common meal anticipates a future eucharist, anticipates eucharist with a small "e" where we can courageously face our fears and witness to the hope within us. By the way, where was Peter? The received text says that Jesus had already appeared to him, but it doesn't sound convincing and it comes to us secondhand. The next story is all about Peter meeting Jesus for the first time after he rose from the dead.

In Galilee by the sea

They were in Galilee by the sea: Peter, Thomas, and Nathanael, with the sons of Zebedee, James and John, and two other disciples. Peter said he was going fishing and they said they would go with him. So they took the boat out onto the sea, but all that night they caught nothing. A little after daybreak, they saw someone standing on the beach. They did not know it was Jesus. He called to them: had they caught any fish? They told him they had nothing. Cast your net to the right of the boat, he said, and so they did. Soon it was so filled to overflowing they could hardly haul it in. Then John said to Peter, it is Jesus! Peter never said a word. Instead, he jumped into the sea to guide the net that was bursting with fish and then helped to drag it ashore. They saw a charcoal fire on the beach. Jesus asked them for some of their fish.

Peter pulled a few from the net and gave the fish to Jesus,
who invited them all to breakfast. Jesus took bread and gave
it to them, and he also gave them some fish. None of them
dared to ask who he was, because they knew it was Jesus.

When they had finished breakfast, Jesus took Peter aside
and asked him if he loved him. Peter replied affirmatively,
insisting, you know that I love you. Three times in all Jesus
asked Peter if he loved him. Three times Peter responded, each
time growing more agitated. You know everything, he said.
You know that I love you. Three times Jesus commissioned
Peter. Feed my lambs. Tend my sheep. Feed my sheep. Then
Jesus said, follow me. (Jn 21:1–17)

⚬≈⚬

The Galilean men had returned home. Peter was among them.
Where else would he be? After denying Jesus a third time,
he left the high priest's courtyard and went weeping into the
night. We hadn't seen him since, although there were dubious
reports that Peter had run to the grave site, that Peter had seen
an empty tomb. The texts are inconclusive. Tradition assumes
that Peter was in Jerusalem with all the other disciples when
Jesus first appeared among them in that upper room, but I am
convinced he was not.

Consider this scenario. It did not make sense for the Galilean men to remain there in the city. They had been identified
as associates of Jesus and could have been apprehended, perhaps even executed, because of their bond with him. It was
much safer for them to go home, and that is what they did.
Peter is in Galilee as our narrative begins. He has gone back
to the water, to do what he had so often done, take comfort

from the sea. He and the sons of Zebedee at one time had been fishermen, and, deep down, they still were.

Jesus was also in Galilee. He had told the women to whom he had appeared that he would be going there, and that Peter and the brothers would be seeing him there. The women would also see him again back in Galilee. Jesus went there ahead of the women because the Galilean men were there and they had not yet seen him. Getting the good news secondhand had not worked well in Jerusalem. It would have been even harder for the Galilean women to have brought the tidings home. Why would the men believe them? So Jesus saw the men before the women returned to tell their story, and, what is vitally important, finally, they saw him. On the shore of the sea of Galilee, they too became eyewitnesses that he had risen from the dead. He gave them what they needed most in order to get their attention: a net full of fish, a bountiful breakfast, and the chance to begin again.

What convinced me that this is the way it was is written right into the story. From the way the men relate to Jesus once they realize it is not some stranger standing there on the shore, it is evident they had not seen him before. Peter must have been mortified. After all, he had denied Jesus, even though he had sworn he would support him to the death. Jesus invites them to a meal. No one gets excited. No one seems happy to see him. They eat their meal in silence. No one asks any questions. Nobody says a word. The ecstatic, overflowing joy characteristic of resurrection meals is starkly, eerily absent. They had been so sure that he was dead. News had not yet reached them, because the women who had stayed in Jerusalem had not yet made it home. The women remained, but the men had fled. It was overwhelming guilt and shame that stifled that breakfast circle. No wonder no one said a word. Had these men met Jesus earlier, they would have already dealt with their denial and their desertion. Traditionally, we stop the story here without examining its implications and then proceed to interpret the situation in ways that explain it away. It is time to simply say what it is. This Galilean breakfast was an awkward, humiliating, miserable moment, especially in the life of Peter, as members of an inner circle are suddenly sitting face to face with the leader they had deserted and a commitment they had betrayed.

Here again is a resurrection meal where Jesus is present with his disciples as they break bread together. Although the tone is somber, the moment is authentic, a snapshot of what life is about and how we can count on Jesus to pursue us like the hound of heaven whenever we run away. This meal is another prototype of eucharist with a small "e." The lesson we learn from this encounter is that there is no sin, no failing, that cannot be forgiven, if only we turn with a contrite heart to seek divine forgiveness by seeking forgiveness of one another and promise to sin no more.

The tension of that which is unresolved compels us to continue on with the story. After breakfast, Jesus took Peter aside to tell him that he loved him and had forgiven him. *Peter, do you love me? Do you know that I love you? Can you forgive and love yourself as I have loved and forgiven you?* The threefold declaration helped his distraught and remorseful friend gain the courage to forgive himself and begin to love again. With this rite of passage came the birth of a new community characterized by an equality that Jesus had proclaimed. Then Jesus commissioned Peter to a new leadership role when he said to him: "Follow me."

⁓

Peter and the Galilean disciples, male and female, returned to Jerusalem and settled into the upper room that had become their meeting place while they were in the city. Jesus appeared another time to the disciples gathered in that room, perhaps again at a meal, but whether it happened before or after the Galileans had returned is difficult to determine. Thomas had not been present the first time Jesus had appeared, and when the disciples told him that they had seen Jesus, he refused to believe them. Until he could see for himself the holes from the nails in the hands of Jesus and touch the devastating wound in his side, he would not believe it. So Jesus returned to turn the doubting Thomas into a believer (Jn 20:24–29). This story, a favorite among people in the pews, represents a dilemma. Thomas was supposedly among those who had been invited to breakfast with Jesus on the Galilean seashore. He could not have been in both places because he could not have seen Jesus for the first time in two different locations. If he had seen Jesus in Galilee, he could not have been the doubting Thomas in the Jerusalem episode. Or, if he did see him for the first time in the upper room, he could not have been a participant in the Galilean breakfast. Both texts refer to him as the "Twin." Perhaps the solution is to place one twin in Jerusalem and another in Galilee. When we tell stories to one another, these are some of the things that emerge to add a spark to our conversations and light a fire in our heart. The Spirit is in the details, and details are open to change.

Imagine what the disciples of Jesus were talking about during mealtime, and at other times, in that upper room. Some of the subjects would have been mundane, but others would have been loftier, just as our own conversations are or can be. They had no idea what they were waiting for or when it was going to happen. Doesn't that sound a lot like us? All they knew was to remain in place until they had been empowered. Perhaps we should do the same.

~ 8 ~

Pentecost and the spirit of Jesus

The disciples were all in that upper room, waiting for some sign of what to do next. Peter and John and James and Andrew, Philip and Thomas, Bartholomew and Matthew, James son of Alphaeus and Simon the Zealot, and Judas the son of James. Mary the mother of Jesus was there. So were his brothers and sisters. So were all those women who were the first eyewitnesses to his resurrection. There were probably others as well. They all knew they would not see him again, for the last time he was with them, he told them he would be going away, and then, suddenly, he was gone.

Pentecost

On Pentecost they were all together with Mary the mother of Jesus when they experienced a sudden rush of wind throughout the room where they were gathered. Their hearts burned within them. Filled with the Holy Spirit, they felt empowered to go into the streets to witness in their own way to the wonderful works of God, women as well as men. Visitors from various cultures who spoke a variety of languages

*heard and understood them, each in their own way. Some,
however, thought they were drunk, but Peter came forward
to defend them, saying, this fulfills the prophecy of how it
will be in the last days when God's Spirit will be given to all,
to slaves as well as to those who are free, to women as well
as men. On that day our young will envision and our elders
will dream dreams, and yes, our daughters will prophesy, for
the Spirit of God will be given to all, to women as well as
men. (Acts 1:14; 2:1–21)*

The opening chapter of the Book of Acts names the men
who were in the room on the day of Pentecost. I used to
wonder why that was necessary — we know their names by
heart — and wish they had named the women instead. But
this was the foundational moment in the life of the newly
emerging church, so they had to record that the founding
fathers were all present and accounted for in light of what
had happened at the time of the crucifixion. While I still feel
it would have been a blessing to know the women by name,
at least we now acknowledge that they too were in the room.
We know the mother of Jesus was there because the Bible
says so. Common sense says, so was her sister, and so were
their daughters and sons. Certainly all those eyewitnesses to
the resurrection of Jesus, the Galilean women and others in
their discipleship circle, and most likely all who had followed
him, or been drawn to him, or been healed by him, their
numbers limited only by the space within the room. Pentecost
was a turning point in the lives and ministries of women, for

the nascent church came into being with women and men together sharing leadership roles.

The spirit of Jesus

Pentecost was a turning point for yet another reason. The Spirit that was received that day was none other than the spirit of Jesus. The Holy Spirit is one spirit, for the spirit of God, the spirit of Jesus, the Holy Spirit are one. That outpouring of Spirit represents a significant shift in focus with regard to the presence of Jesus, away from a physical/visible presence to an ongoing presence in spirit in the heart of the community. That spirit would now be with and among all his followers, merging with their own spirits and felt from time to time like a fire deep within. From that day forward women and men, young and old, rich and poor, Jew and Gentile would embody the mission of Jesus they were committed to carrying on. This empowerment of Spirit resulted in the birth of a new creation, an egalitarian movement of ordinary people whose stark individuality would coalesce as one.

The following conclusions emerge from our reflection on eucharist with a small "e" during the life of the historical Jesus and the time between his death and Pentecost and from our brief consideration of eucharist in the apostolic church.

Two streams of eucharist exist. One of them is eucharist with a small "e" and the other is Eucharist.

❧

A tradition of small "e" eucharist can be discerned in the life of Jesus. The Tradition's Sacrament of the Eucharist has been shaped by the life of the church.

❧

Small "e" eucharist considers all recorded meals in the life of Jesus. Eucharist looks to the supper understood to be his last.

❧

What small "e" eucharist remembers is the entire life of Jesus. Large "E" remembers the death of Jesus until he comes again.

❧

The presence of Jesus in both is real. In small "e" eucharist this real presence is a spirit presence within the community and in the hearts of individuals. In Eucharist this real presence is a physical presence or a symbolic presence in the elements of bread and wine.

❧

Celebrants for small "e" eucharist are the priesthood of all believers. Celebrants for the Eucharist are those who are recipients of a sacramental ordination.

❧

Resurrection appearances are a bridge between these two streams. On the one hand, they form a continuity with what has gone before, as Jesus interacts with his disciples in the context of a meal. On the other hand, they prepare the way for what is still to come.

෴

Eucharist with a small "e" continues within the Jerusalem church, so that small "e" is part of the larger Tradition in Christianity's formative stages. Characteristics that will distinguish the shape of Eucharist in the Western world emerge in Gentile territory, in Corinth, with Paul. The Jerusalem and Corinth communities represent two eucharistic types in the early church. Sometime after the fourth century, only Eucharist remains, although the development differs in the East and in the West.

෴

Pentecost marks the beginning of the Christian church in Spirit. It is also a decisive turning point with regard to the presence of Jesus. His physical presence, his appearances in resurrected form, give way to a spirit presence. From now on he will be present in Spirit, really and truly present in Spirit, whenever the community gathers. His gift to this community is a new way of seeing and being in the world. The followers of Jesus, now one in the Spirit, will also embody the presence of Christ out there in the midst of the world in every generation.

PART THREE

Celebrating eucharist with a small "e"

∾

Opening Up to the Spirit

~ 9 ~

Making all things new

You inspire us to envision
all the fullness of shalom
on a new path through tradition
that will surely lead us home.

It is so simple, even a child can do it. In fact, a child should
do it, celebrate eucharist with a small "e." It may well be the
best way to introduce something new. A child is unencumbered by the baggage that inhibits. A child would have no
trouble believing that Jesus is really present, as real as that
child's imaginary friend who eludes adult detection. A child
would also understand that what we do in church on Sunday
is different from what we do at home all the other days of the
week. At picnics and parties, snack times and meals, celebrating eucharist with family and friends whenever and wherever
is a sacrament all its own.

A sacrament forms an intrinsic bond between our tangible,
embodied world and the invisible world of spirit and does so
through visible things. Sacramental metaphors link the am-
biguous here and now to that which is beyond us, giving us
a more comprehensive sense of what it is we are searching
for and where we are likely to find it. Sacramental moments

mark those inner and outer realities that have a lasting value, suggesting and sometimes clarifying what God desires of us. More often than not they are for us a bridge over troubled waters into the pacifying presence of the One who makes all things new.

There are many pathways to and from the sanctuary of the heart. How precious are those that, step by step, lead to an inner light. Maps designed to take us there are written in ritual language. Eucharist is ritual. The more we celebrate eucharist in the midst of what is familiar, the more we are bound to feel at home with the many metaphors and meanings that eucharist employs. Eucharist with a small "e" is ritual for everyday living, for ordinary folk like you and me living ordinary lives. What is meant here is not a fully developed rite or service, except perhaps now and then. Eucharist with a small "e" is more like a ritual interlude that renders whatever we do together — the meal itself, our conversation, the quality of our interactions — sacred and sanctifying.

At the heart of small "e" eucharist is a theology of access and accessibility. Access means the act of coming toward or near, a way or a means of approaching. It is the right to enter, the right to be admitted. It is the right to come in. The same holds for the word "accessible," only from the other side. That which is accessible can be approached or entered, is easy to approach or enter, is open to whomever comes near and wants to come in. Words such as these become theological when speaking of the Divine. God is so approachable, the spirit of God so accessible, the spirit of Jesus eternally waiting for the hesitant to come near. We gain access to the love we crave when we enter the place where love waits in hiding or is boldly displayed. We gain access to forgiveness when we dare to cross the threshold of that line drawn in the sand. We gain access to the largesse of grace when we open up to the Spirit. Ask, we are told, and it will be given to you. Seek, and you will find. Knock, and the door will be opened to you (Mt 7:7). All it takes is initiative to rendezvous with God.

A theology of access is for everyone. Moreover, we are expected to be fluent on either side. We have to be accessible so others can come in. We have to be approachable so strangers can come near. Our hearts and minds have to be open and not be resistant to change. Accessibility means accommodation to another's distinctiveness. It means seeing how our deepest values appear from the other side. Another's pain, another's despair has a right to be given access to our life-restoring resources, limited though they be. Access is not just for insiders anymore. It is a basic theological right that flows from the heart of Jesus. As such it is a life force capable of transforming a socially and politically inaccessible world. It can and will be ritually transmitted, if our approach to ritual is right.

In one sense eucharist with a small "e" is not really about Jesus but what Jesus was about. What were his issues, his main concerns? How might we champion similar causes and make what was his our own? What was his real passion? I don't mean here that final countdown of crucifying pain. I mean the consuming focus of all those other months of days. A closer look will tell us his energy was directed toward those denied access to what was rightfully theirs. Eucharist with a small "e" gives us an opportunity to talk about these things, to apply them to our own locale and the world that extends beyond it, to make some resolutions to do what Jesus might have done, to know in the way that lovers know who it is that sustains them.

Eucharist with a small "e" is not oriented toward the endtime and the afterlife to come. It is turned toward our wounded world with eyes wide open, to announce with actions that speak louder than words that the transforming spirit of a loving God is already here among us and that all have equal access to this source of empowerment. This is the core theological thrust of small "e" eucharist. We are more concerned with here than we are with the hereafter, and vitally concerned that what we cherish will still be here a long time after we have had enough of war and planetary degradation. Jesus came to renew and transform religion and society, saying, behold, I make all things new (Rev 21:5). This is a powerful mantra. All radical systemic change begins with a change in perspective. This fundamental shift in seeing leads to countless incremental changes that will add up in the end. People working together, doing whatever needs to be done, can and will make the difference. The spirit of Jesus, God's spirit, who makes the impossible possible, will see that it is enough.

Making all things new in and through the spirit of Jesus includes reimagining themes that are core to eucharistic tradition and definitive of small "e" eucharist. We do this to become more like the One who was also one of us, remembering the life he lived each time his Spirit comes again.

~ 10 ~

Giving thanks

Thank You, God, for the gift of birth,
for love made flesh to refresh the earth.
For life and strength and length of days,
we give You thanks and praise.

How often do we take time each day to thank God for our blessings? Let's be honest. Not often enough, for life itself is a blessing. All that we have and all that we are we receive from our Creator. An attitude of gratitude should in fact define us, but that is not the case. Isn't it time for a change? How about a year-round resolution to shift from forgetfulness or habitual indifference to a daily routine of intermittent thankfulness and praise.

Eucharist with a small "e" establishes a climate where to give thanks is the norm, for *eucharistia* is thanksgiving. The term, derived from the Greek, means an attitude of thankfulness and its outward expression. The word itself indicates the nature of the action. To celebrate eucharist is to give thanks mindfully and meaningfully and in a visible way for all the wonderful works of God. From the depths of our lived reality — for what was and is and is to be — in celebrating small "e" eucharist, we give thanks to God.

The root word in *eucharistia* or "eucharist" is *charis,* which means gift or grace. A charism is a special gift given by the Spirit to an individual or a community. It is a dynamic and formative word in religious communities of women and men striving to embody the special charism the spirit of God has entrusted to them as their mission to the world. The gift of healing, the gift of teaching, the gift of perpetual adoration, the gift of justice-based advocacy and action on behalf of those oppressed, the gift to leave one's home to live and serve in another culture — these are contemporary expressions of what Paul refers to so eloquently in his first letter to the Corinthian community (chap. 12). He speaks of the many gifts of the Spirit manifested within the community bound together by eucharist. There are different gifts but one Spirit who activates each charism for the benefit of all.

Another word derived from eucharist is "charisma," whose reality is elusive. Charisma is a special spirit. We know it when we see it. The contemporary definition of charisma is, first of all, a gift of God's grace, and second, a special quality of leadership that captivates the imagination. In a certain sense, each of us has been gifted with charisma, for each of us, believe it or not, captivates the imagination of God. When we give thanks for the gifts we are given, when we give thanks for the gift that we are to ourselves and one another, we celebrate small "e" eucharist. Because each of us is a gift of the Spirit, because we channel Spirit gifts and graces to the world around us, we are living eucharist, and for this we give thanks and praise.

Thanksgiving, a national holiday, is a designated time set aside each year for the purpose of giving thanks collectively for our many blessings. Sunday services are opportunities to give thanks to God each week. A domestic eucharist with a small "e" provides us with the means for thanks giving every day. When the negative thrust of our daily news threatens to overwhelm us with catastrophic carnage and unmitigated pain, a eucharistic setting helps us see there is also grace and goodness where we least expect to find it. These are the moments for giving voice to unexpressed thankfulness. It may be hard to say sometimes, but we really need to do it. "What do you say?" we prod the child who has just been given something. And we insist on the right response, a simple, spoken, thank you. We diligently teach our children what we fail to put into practice in any consistent way. Graces and blessings permeate our lives. What difference might it make if we were to whisper to ourselves throughout each day: "Child of God, what do you say?"

We thank you, God, for the rising sun and its promise of a new beginning...for the air we breathe, the food we eat, the dreams that refuse to die...for a place in the world of the living and a faith in what lies beyond it...for horizons that keep moving away and the desire to follow after...for a vision too big to handle alone and for all those who embrace it...for words that sing and songs that speak and the syncopated rhythms of nature's music making...for children ...for elderly folk...for all who inhabit this planet...for the rainbow of possibilities in the coloring book of creation...for peace wherever we find it...or whenever we feel it...for all the ways we believe in love's capacity to heal...for all who refuse to give up on hope...for all that we have failed to see or forgotten to say: thank you, God our Creator.

~ 11 ~

Sacramental meal

The poor will have privilege, the hungry will eat.
All of the homeless will dance in the street.
In God's revelation, real love will release
the reincarnation of justice and peace.

It was pitch dark in the tents that night. No moon came to compensate for the lack of electricity or the shortage of kerosene lanterns. Several hundred people huddled expectantly in the shadows of this camp for emaciated children. Tiny bodies, listless and limp, lay in the arms of scrawny adults, waiting patiently. I made my final rounds for the day, distributing food to the hungry, mindful of the priestly connotations associated with taking and breaking the bread of life. No worry here about special garb or the precise nature of the elements, no time for formulaic phrases or ritual relevance. High protein biscuits now, soybean porridge in the morning, sweet powdered milk laced with oil for midday and early evening, and if the supply truck comes tomorrow, a small, infrequent banana. Give us this day our daily bread, I prayed when I rose that morning. Once again a merciful God heard and answered my prayer. I gave thanks for this extraordinary grace and then made my way back to base camp, leaving behind a suffering people eating a sacramental meal in the middle of the night.

Some of my most memorable meals took place in makeshift refugee camps far away from home. I came face to face with famine that summer in Ethiopia, and before that, in the sprawling camps along the Thai-Cambodian border among traumatized survivors of the Pol Pot regime. I learned what it means to be hungry, really and truly hungry, and what a significant blessing it is when that hunger is assuaged. After those searing experiences, the eucharist, for me, has never been the same. I came to realize that eucharist is at the very core of life wherever it is happening and reveals itself in our efforts to attend to another's needs. Celebrating small "e" eucharist in the daily unfolding of our lives can make us aware of hunger in all its manifestations. Putting a meal on the table can be a microcosmic reminder that a world waits to be fed. Hunger rages somewhere in the world in every generation. We need not travel far today to encounter hungry people. They walk the streets of our cities, huddle alone in nursing homes, are locked behind prison walls. An outrageous number of children go to bed hungry every night. Hunger is rampant in so many forms. Hunger for food, hunger for survival, hunger for justice, freedom, mercy, hunger for companionship and an everlasting hunger for love. How do we respond to hunger when we are confronted by it? How do we face the hunger in our loved ones and in ourselves?

Take.... Break.... words with mnemonic power, a power invested in them over centuries of repetition. Take bread.

Break bread. The words evoke eucharist. In a sacramental setting outside the Sacrament, these words bring sacred content
into our secular contexts, carry with them the capacity for
transformational change. The word "take" is burdened with a
bundle of associations, positive and otherwise. We hear it in
so many contexts: don't take it personally . . . don't take the
last piece of cake . . . take your little sister . . . take it on the
chin. The word dances wildly through our vocabulary: take
courage . . . take cover . . . take charge . . . take a chance . . . take
lessons . . . take pity . . . take heed . . . take heart . . . take precau-
tions . . . take a breather . . . take a number . . . take a walk . . .
take it easy . . . take ten . . . take turns . . . take me! In a society
prone to takeout, this word is ripe for bridge-building between
the secular and the sacred at a small "e" eucharist meal. As
our spirituality deepens around our kitchen tables, we begin
to take responsibility, to take notice of the little things, take
seriously what we would once have dismissed, heed the urge
to take action or take part in an initiative on someone else's
behalf. We take time to listen. We take time to take care of
ourselves. We take stock. We take a break. We take and break
the bread of compassion and are suddenly acutely aware of all
that has been broken: broken homes, broken hearts, broken
promises, and the shards of broken dreams. Yet the grace of
a sacramental meal reminds us as well of daybreak, when the
shadows we dread are all dispelled. We experience a break-
through at those times when on the verge of breaking down
we are unexpectedly delivered, or when in the midst of de-
privation we fortuitously feel fulfilled. Break the good news,
O Holy One. Tell us that eucharist happens in circumstances
such as these.

Life exists through processes that are similar to a meal. To nourish and be nourished, consume and be consumed, feed and be fed are fundamental to the universe. The fiery forces in outer space feed into the birth of new and expanding galaxies. Wind feeds and fans the flame, rain reinvigorates the barren ground, sunlight sustains vegetation, giving energy for seeds to form and flower in a cycle of life that never ends, vegetation sustains other species, and life within other species is maintained by feeding oneself and one another. The universe is really one gigantic sacramental meal, a cosmic eucharist. To those who have eyes to see it as such, signs and symbols abound, encouraging us to reconsider our own place and our own role at this universal table.

What if somebody asked you to name your own most memorable meal? How would you respond? Was it the first time you nursed your newborn baby? Perhaps it was the candlelight dinner when your beloved proposed ... or the big birthday party that caught you by surprise ... or that sumptuous Thanksgiving meal when everyone made it home ... or the victory banquet with the team ... or the barbeque to celebrate a safe return from war ... or that anniversary breakfast, so special after so many years. Each of these occasions is a sacramental meal, defining for us in manifold ways the meaning of communion. Sacramental meals, sacramental moments permeate our lives, whether or not we know it. To know is to be receptive to the force of each meal's blessings and to be nurtured by the memory of that moment or that meal.

It is good to come together for a meal with those who are close to us. It is also essential to invite to our table those beyond our inner circle, if we would change the dynamic of a xenophobic world. The meals we share with family and friends, with the passerby, with strangers, are like the table fellowship of Jesus. They are eucharist with a small "e," where we break the bread of accessibility, one bite at a time.

~ 12 ~

Real presence

I love You for the permanence of Your being.
In You there is no question of goodbye.
And everything that interrupts my seeing
is but the love reflected in Your eye.

We are obsessed with location, with space, place, and bound-
aries. You stay on your side. I'll stay on mine. We put up walls,
figurative and real, to restrain and contain the other — the
alien, the stranger, the enemy, those of another culture or
class, those of another religion. We even do this to God. Be-
ware of strange gods, we are warned, meaning, stay away from
that which is beyond our understanding, which, theologically
speaking, is the very meaning of God. Where is God? Everywhere. Well, yes, but not exactly, for we have been taught
that the real God is located within our own religion. Defined,
described, circumscribed — God is here and everywhere, but
not really "over there."

The God from whom all life has emerged cannot be con-
tained by force of will or definition. God is the first to break
our rules, residing in those "godless" places where we say God
cannot go. Primitive peoples long ago worshiped God in nature, attributing to a sacred presence all that was essential to

life. Indeed, the Divine Presence permeates everything, extending to the far reaches of the cosmos and beyond. If we were truly convinced of this, we could access that power for good in a cooperative enterprise. However, it is hard for some to see God where authority says God isn't, but we need to do it anyway. How else to liberate God from those canonical restrictions that limit access to the Divine and Divinity's approach to us? How else to liberate us from the theological prejudice that has led us into so many wars and spawns discriminatory behavior? Theology may seek to determine what is real and relevant, but the manifold manifestations of God have never followed our rules. Theophany, an experience of God, precedes theology, because experience is or ought to be prior to its interpretation. Whoever people say God is, whatever the name or image we attribute to the Divine, does not in any way limit the reality of God. But this must also be said. God who is real and really present may not be real or really present to me through certain images or names. Therefore, it is essential that we trust our own experience of God, who is beyond all names and transcends every one of our images even while inhabiting them. The important thing to remember is that God is most real to us when we are in a loving and intimate relationship with the Divine.

During eucharist with a small "e," we enter into relationship with God through the real presence of Jesus, not a physical presence but a spirit really present, the spirit of the risen Jesus, the spirit of the cosmic Christ. The spirit of Jesus is a holy Spirit who abides with us forever, whose presence transcends the physical limits of time, space, even the complex theological systems we have constructed. Our Easter liturgy may focus on the embodied Jesus come back to life, but Easter is essentially a celebration of spirit. The really good news of Easter is that the spirit of the One whom God raised up is the spirit of the living God.

Mary Magdalene was the first to see the resurrected Jesus. Already in the spirit realm, he revealed his presence to her in the form she knew him by. She reached out to him in ecstatic joy, anticipating a physical embrace, but Jesus said, "Do not cling to me," for he had already passed over to the other side. He was beyond the finite, yet here he was, present in spirit, to speak a liberating word. This is the word he would say to us. Do not get too attached to my physical manifestation. There is a time for letting go. The way it was can no longer be. Something substantial has changed. Cling to the memory, it will nourish you, but embrace reality.

The encounter between Jesus and Mary Magdalene has significant meaning for us, for it is about an abiding relationship confronting a heartrending change. Many of us know all too well that to lose someone we dearly love means losing a physical presence. What we sometimes fail to realize is that it also means opening ourselves to another mode of presence that may be deeper and far more penetrating than the one we knew before. The living, loving presence in spirit of someone we cherish, of God whom we love, is a gift beyond all imagining, a presence that is truly real. This is the message of Easter. I will be with you always. The disciples took that farewell promise of Jesus on faith, but now we know it is true. Jesus would no longer be seen as he was or in the way he had been before, but experienced in a whole new way, accessible to all.

However we explain it to ourselves, Jesus is really risen and no longer bound by the limitations of a physical universe. The risen Christ transcends such things as gender, race, religion — a prototype of the unique integration of embodiment and spirit, of the divine and human aspects inherent in all God's children. The Risen One is everywhere, in the face of compassion, the work of justice, the spirit of shalom, wherever goodness overflows and love is made manifest. The spirit of the risen Jesus is now the spirit of the risen Christ always with us and within us, present in the form of intuitive wisdom, imagination, and risk. Understood in this way, we too will feel the spirit of Jesus really present, lifting our spirits, engendering hope, teaching us to trust more and more that invisible world of the spirit, where we too will one day dwell.

There is something else that must be said about a presence that is real. The spirit of Jesus may be with me, real and really present, but may not be really present to me. Recall the times someone said to you in the midst of a conversation: "Excuse me, but where are you?" Or, "Where have you just been?" Something about the way we are says to the other, you are physically here, but the core of you is elsewhere. As we go through life we find that we are physically with many people in all kinds of situations, but seldom really present. Even with family members. Sometimes it isn't necessary to be totally attentive. We are not expected to be relational when sitting on a bus. But it is a quality that is absolutely essential at times, to be really present to another, to allow another person to be really present to me.

Eucharist with a small "e" is all about developing a quality of presence in a meaningful, relational way. The key is focused

attention. That which was at the periphery becomes the center of attention or the subject of our concern. Others who
are with me are suddenly one with me. I am fully aware of
them and they are aware of me. We are present to each other.
I invoke the spirit of Jesus who is then really present to me.
The presence of Jesus in small "e" eucharist is a real presence
in spirit, but is really present to us only when we intentionally
make it so.

One final consideration. Even when we are really present,
is the person who is present real? Is that the *real* me, without
my masks, without all the smoke and mirrors, the pretenses,
the posturing, the roles I sometimes play? The labels others lay
on me, the images others may have of me, the negative image
I might have of myself often prevent others from knowing who
I really am, prevent me from really knowing myself and from
fulfilling my potential. False starts and false pretenses too often
take too much of our time on our way to becoming real. Love,
however, when it is real, reaches down to the core. When we
love someone, when we are loved, then we are really real. May
small "e" eucharist, over time, be a safe place, a welcoming
place for the real me and the real you to be really present to
each other in spirit and in truth.

— 13 —

This is my body

We are drops of Living Water,
we are branches of the Vine.
We are bread and body broken,
we are chalice for the Wine.

The first person to utter the words we associate with Jesus must have been his mother. For nine months they were one body, Mary and her child. Like any mother, surely she said of the new life taking form within her: this is my body! She would also have watched her newborn baby nursing at her breast and marveled: his is *my* body, his is *my* blood, bone of my bone, flesh of my flesh. Mary alone can identify with the physical body of Jesus. To her we owe the embodied presence of Jesus in our world.

A majority of the miracles of Jesus had something to do with the body. He cured those burning up with fever or suffering from disease. He healed those who were blind or deaf or unable to walk unassisted. He touched the bodies of the ritually unclean, although it was forbidden, including the bodies of those who had died and those who were labeled sinners. He reached out to those who were broken either in body or in spirit and made them whole again. The woman caught in adultery, the woman with the flow of blood, the woman who came to anoint his feet, individuals possessed by evil spirits, lepers, and other outcasts were touched by him and changed. He fed the hungry, spoke out on behalf of those who were being treated unjustly, and was deeply concerned that the burdens of the poor might be more than they could bear. He embodied God's spirit and had a significant impact on the lives of the oppressed.

This is my body, Jesus said, at what was to be his last supper, words that are central to Eucharist in the tradition of the church. The phrase and its parallel, *This is my blood,* are spoken over the bread and wine in the Sacrament of the Eucharist in imitation of what Jesus did on the night before he died. They mark the precise moment when the eucharistic elements become the Body and Blood of Christ in Roman Catholic tradition. As we have already seen, our sacramental Eucharist evolved to this understanding. Prior to this development, Christ's presence in the early church was perceived to be in the community eating and drinking together. During the course of their common meal, the community was transformed by the Holy Spirit into the body of Christ.

What could have been the impetus for the church to make such a claim? Consider this scenario. When Jesus said, *This is my body,* wouldn't it make a world of difference to know where he was looking? Christian art and Christian tradition fix his gaze on the bread and the cup. However, he could have been looking directly at his disciples as he offered them the bread, saying to those who were gathered around him: this is my body — yes, you are my body — an extension of my spirit, a continuation of my mission. Soon I will have no body but yours to carry on the work of God, to proclaim the good news of God's reign already here among us.

It would have been revolutionary, such a radical reinterpretation of a traditional blessing. Far more than a metaphorical association is implied. We saw in our brief visit to Corinth how participants at a meal in the context of a Eucharist were told to act in a way that reflected that they were the body of Christ. This identification with Christ's body is foundational to the early church. The concept of the community as an extension of the body of Christ continued throughout Christian history and on into the present, giving credibility to the claim that Jesus is its source.

As members of Christ's mystical body, we are charged to put on Christ, to clothe ourselves with Christlike virtues and behave in an appropriate way. Celebrating eucharist with a small "e" will help us to habituate this and make it relevant. When we gather to tell our stories, we include not only positive accounts but also incidents of disembodiment crying out for redemption: physical needs, spiritual needs, systemic insensitivity, hearts on the verge of breaking, lives in need of healing. Our world today is far too cavalier in regard to how we treat our bodies. The bodies of women are flaunted to entice the bombarded consumer and used by far too many men solely for physical pleasure. The violence inflicted on the bodies of women and the bodies of our children, the number of women and girls who truly dislike their bodies and want to make them over, the countless bodies blown to bits in so many senseless wars, the bodies we have put to death in state-approved executions indicate a disconnect with seeing our humanity as the extended body of Christ. It is a paradox. We who proclaim our love for Jesus crucify Christ's body again and again through our inhumanity.

We are the body of Christ when we open ourselves to the spirit of Jesus and continue what he began. But let us be very careful that we do not limit Jesus. The one who welcomed everyone left us a challenging perspective as our legacy. He identified with those who are hungry and thirsty and lack proper clothes, with the sick, the felon, the stranger, saying: when we attend to their bodily needs, when we give food, drink, clothing, care, compassion, empathy, shelter, we are doing these things for him. Christ's body is one with embodied humanity. Here then is real presence. Here is his body. Here is his blood. Indeed, if we would be brutally honest, here among suffering humanity is authentic eucharist. And do remember this. Jesus was not talking about ministering only to Christians. He did not say tend to those who share our religious affiliation. He referred to all humanity when he said that we will be judged on how we respond to those in need. We tend to ignore those we consider "others" and focus instead on our own. Christ is telling us otherwise. The "other" is also, in our own times, an embodiment of Christ.

Look into the face of the other — hungry, ill, lonely, depressed — and see the face of the spirit of Jesus incarnate once again. Then look beyond at the wider world, to the trees, the rivers, the clouds and the stars, to the snapdragons and the fireflies, to the prairies and the hillside slopes rainforest green in the sun, and give thanks for the gift of embodiment. This is *my* body, Spirit says. The universe is sacred Presence, embodiment of the Divine.

– 14 –

Do this

When we do this, we remember,
it is Jesus we remember,
feel his Spirit and remember
God is love.

Do what? What are we to do? I think we already know. What did Jesus tell us to do? Feed the hungry, assuage another's thirst, welcome the stranger, visit the sick. The real question is, then, how and when will we do the things we know need to be done?

We begin with an assessment. Identify who is suffering and what they are suffering from. Who around you is hungry? What is that person hungering for? Is the person or family in need of food? That you can do something about, either through a local food bank or directly, door to door. Help one child go to bed at night without an empty stomach. Do this. Just do it. That child, like so many others, is living in our own neighborhood and we don't even know it. Find out about it, be better informed, and everything else will follow.

Start locally and bring to it a wider, more global perspective. Begin with basic physical needs, but do not ignore the others. There are those who hunger for compassion or for companionship, for someone to tell their story to, someone who will listen to them and ultimately accept them. There is so much we can do in memory of Jesus when we call upon his Spirit to come and accompany us. Gather your family, call on some friends, reflect on this together. Share some food, and there you are, celebrating small "e" eucharist.

When we do this, we are doing what Jesus would have done. We do this in memory of him, remembering the life he lived in such a way that he lives it again through us. Ritual — eucharist with a small "e" — is a means for reorienting our lives, so that we might live our lives in memory of him. *Do this in memory of me* takes on a whole new meaning for us, for it is linked to mission and our multiple ministries. We look to the life of Jesus and then redirect our own. The world needs us to do much more to ensure its survival, needs us to act compassionately to all who are perilously close to falling into oblivion. Theologically, as we do this, we also hold in living memory the crucified body of Jesus, for we minister to those who, in their wounds, bear the stigmata of Christ.

The prophetic mission of Jesus is for us the interpretive key. When we hear the words, "do this," before we consider what it is we should do, stop and consider,

What would Jesus do?

There is a worldwide crisis regarding the rampant spread of AIDS, which is pandemic in Africa and is devastating a number of large and densely populated areas of the world where drugs that can alleviate suffering cost more than any can afford.

What would Jesus do?

A booming sex trade blatantly exploits women and children for profit and pleasure all around the globe and sexual deviates violate the sanctuaries of young bodies, even in the sanctuaries of our churches here at home.

What would Jesus do?

People in nursing homes nationwide are no longer able to provide for themselves, have no one at all to visit them, have nothing but their memories to comfort and sustain them.

What would Jesus do?

A single mother with three jobs lives from paycheck to paycheck, with never enough to provide sufficient food and clothes for her children.

What would Jesus do?

A neighbor who is housebound and living alone enjoys visitors, loves to talk, but is repetitive and boring.

What would Jesus do?

We are often too busy or too tired to spend quality time with family and friends doing things that are frivolous and fun.

What would Jesus do?

Scripture reminds us to *do* the word and not just sit around listening to it (James 1:22). If we really hear the word of God, we will translate that word into action. The most effective action occurs when we become the word we would do, the word we would put into action. If I would do justice, as God

commands, then I need to begin by being just in my interactions with others. If I would engage in works of compassion,
first I must be compassionate or strive to grow in compassion
through the compassionate work I do. We sow seeds of love
best simply by being loving. Eucharist with a small "e" provides us with opportunities to relate what we hear to what we
do in memory of Jesus. As God's word becomes flesh in us in
and through the Spirit, we gain access to the deeper meaning
underlying all that we do in memory of Jesus. We share in his
mission to make all things new through an integration of the
sacred and secular aspects of our lives.

~ 15 ~

At-one-ment

Everywhere
Your web of life
gives witness to imagination,
echoing Your whispered word proclaiming
that all are one.

When I looked up at the star-studded sky in the summertime
of my childhood, I never imagined more than a metaphorical
affinity with our Milky Way. The glittering canopy hovering
above marked the end of the universe then. Today it is just
the beginning, and I can say with scientific certainty that I
am made of stardust, for the fundamental elements of life are
an integral part of us all.

What an exhilarating feeling, to be drawn into the Spiral
Galaxy, to play within the Pleiades, to pray in the Planetary
Nebula, to traverse the rings of Saturn, to be traveler and
lover of light and energy from the fingertips of Divine Imagination trillions of light years away, to know in the way that
mystics know, that all of this is not apart from me but is in
fact a part *of* me and one with what is within me.

I was able to make a transition to the full embrace of the
mystical through a paradigm shift in understanding about the

world we live in. Scientists and scholars, and eventually pioneers in spirituality and theology, rethought and rearticulated the nature and scope of the cosmos and the place of our universe within it. Such a profound and fundamental shift affects all aspects of our lives — the way we think, what we believe, how we relate to each other, how we relate to God — or at least it ought to. Most people are unaware of the fact that unseen forces shape and influence all that is made manifest and the manner of our own evolving. While I can talk easily about this now, it took years for a full awakening.

I grew up in a tightly structured world that was more or less predictable. I knew what I was supposed to do, was aware of what I ought to believe, knew who had authority and the consequences of daring to question what everyone seemed to take for granted. Until one of us walked on the moon, outer space and what was out there had no earthly relevance. A vast and empty void separated planet Earth from everything else, or so it was believed. Then Earth was introduced as Gaia, a living, breathing organism with a life force of its own. Suddenly, those who had eyes to see saw things differently. Power, position, relationship are no longer approached the same way when considered through this worldview. Nevertheless, it will take some time for certain things to change.

Species are still ranked according to what is considered most significant down to the least among us, with humanity at the top of the ladder and males accorded the pinnacle of power with dominion over all in most situations. This hierarchic, patriarchal order once attributed to divine intent is still being reflected back onto God. A dualistic separation of sacred and secular, human and divine, human and animal/plant/

mineral, male and female, rich and poor, educated and illiterate, white and colored, powerful and powerless, first world and third world, in and out, us and them is still to a large extent the norm, although it is slowly changing. Separate and divided. Set apart and over against. My God, not your God. If God is on my side, and surely God is, God cannot be on yours. No wonder so many still think that diversity means divisive. In the dominant worldview of my past, the whole consisted of discrete parts in every facet of reality, from the building blocks of organic life to our social and religious constructs. A segmented perspective provided the formative blueprint for our segregated lives. Then along came quantum theory.

There is no such thing as empty space. Beneath the surface of what can be seen, pulsating fields of energy link visible reality and all in between in a dynamic and invisible web of cosmic interconnectedness. Particles and waves move vibrantly in and out of relationship in a subatomic interchange, engaged in a perpetual dance of life, carrying the memory of linkages beyond distant horizons and bearing within the capacity for systemic transformation. In other words, there is no cosmic basis for anyone bowling alone or for an excessive individualism or systemic alienation. The isolated, supersized ego that has gotten us into global wars and leans toward privatization is really an aberration and a threat to species survival. The universe and our biospheres are oriented toward wholeness and not toward segmentation. Swiftly, in ways we will never perceive, neutrinos move in and out of us. Those basic building blocks of life in people and rocks and trees and birds, elements of everything in creation move through us, around us, and back into us in a stunning interchange, so that in some deep and incomprehensible manner, a part of you is a part of me. We are all part of each other. We are all an integral part of the universe, one with the One who created the universe. Truly, we are all one.

Quantum theory is a rich resource for reimagining our relationship with God and with one another. It is the terrain of those who know that the only thing that will save us is a new and unified vision of humanity and our world. That vision needs to be rooted in a theology of innerconnectedness, one that puts God in the midst and not way out there in the distance. It is only as part of the web weaving us all together in the one God that we can come to love one another, share the burdens of one another, be at peace with one another. An apocalyptic vision of the rapture? Yes, but not only of the endtime. It is the vision of Jesus, proclaiming that the reign of God is already here among us. "On that day," says Jesus, speaking of both then and now, "you will know that I am in God and you in me and I in you" (Jn 14:20). Jesus is saying, you will know that we are part of one another.

Mystics throughout the ages have perceived the Divine Presence permeating everything. Our agenda for this third millennium is to learn to live in harmony with all God's people. The first step toward achieving this ultimate imperative is to realize that all of us *are* God's people. Small "e" eucharist celebrates this universal spirit. It promotes a theology of at-one-ment as articulated here in rudimentary form, an understanding rooted in a primal intuition that we are all one.

~ 16 ~

Story

Who am I to sing of glory?
Who am I to sing of praise?
What do I know of the story of
Your strange, mysterious ways?

Life is one long story. As it was, as it is, as it will be. The narrative quality of human experience is reason enough for us to claim storytelling as our birthright. Before anyone put pen to page, everything worth knowing came by word of mouth. That is still true for some even now, and for me in certain circles. To tell is multidimensional, even when the story falls flat. Because storytelling embodies the story, it can convey levels of meaning in a variety of ways.

Scripture is a compendium of stories, from its initial words, "In the beginning," to its final word, "Amen!" Like the stories we tell of ourselves and our friends, the narratives are somewhat disconnected and the myths sometimes hard to believe. In regard to biblical traditions, these span a lengthy period of time and include countless communities. The thread that weaves them together is the belief that their collective story reflects the story of God. It is hard for us to imagine the real life stories behind these texts, for the juice was squeezed out

144

of them when they were formatted for a page. The sacred stories behind sacred texts captured so much more of life than the written word can tell. As chronicle, the texts do not tell all, but that was not their purpose. As inspirational resource, they remain a blessing. The spirit of Jesus urges us to bring our own experience to those sacred stories underlying our sacred texts. So the good news of the Gospel can take the shape of our own times. So the stories of past generations begin to look like our own stories, and the struggles of past populations seem similar to our own. It is hard to see ourselves in stories framed for another time, harder still to imagine that a primary point of those stories was that we tell stories of our own, for our collective story mirrors the story of God.

In principle this should be easy to do. We tell stories all the time. Stories are how we respond to the question: "Tell me, how was your day?" Little kids learn during show and tell just how to engage the listener, what elements are essential, how simple it is to stand up there and say what you have to say. Stories are why cell phone sales have rocketed through the roof. Who cares if what we share is inane or frightfully repetitious. In our ever-unfolding story, whether through chit chat or at times, thank God, through coherent conversation, who we are and what we think and what we really care about is spoken into the universe and, in some sense, will live on. Storytelling can be a filter. What we select, what we let fall away, does not always give an indication of what is really most vital to us, for we often obsess over trivial things and overlook what really counts. Sharing the details, talking it through is also a way of filtering the pain that comes with being slighted, or misunderstood, or maligned. Theater has written the book on such things, and plays that are most successful often mirror ordinary life. What we need to do is connect some dots, for biblical stories, theater plots, and the ups and downs of our own life journey come from a common source. These differing genres inform one another. When we use the experience of one to uncover wisdom in another, we are often doubly blest.

That last point reminds me of a story. I was teaching a course on biblical women to inmates at the women's state prison. I had chosen to talk about the parable of the wise and foolish women and their lamps, not only because it had relevance, but I wanted to hear what the women had to say about that story. I asked them to consider what it meant to be labeled either wise or foolish and what they thought of its use in the text. The parable was told and then retold when one of the women broke in and said that the story had it all wrong. The wise were not really wise at all. Yes! I said to myself, anticipating her response. Then she said, "Those wise women were stupid. Anybody here knows, if you have something, and somebody else wants what you have, you don't fall asleep, because when you wake up, they have what you had, and you are left with nothing."

Telling stories is contagious, for one story leads to another. Not so long ago there was a special event in the prison chapel. I had the privilege of awarding a doctor of ministry degree to the chaplain, something that had never happened there before, for something that had not been done before. Laurie had created an interfaith community within the prison complex that would prepare women to return to society with a more informed understanding of other faith traditions as well as their own. Quite a few people had been invited to this significant event, including the women who had been participants in the project. There were refreshments after the ceremony, which presented a dilemma. Laurie had decided on a menu that would mean something to the women who ate only prison food. Coffee was eliminated in favor of ice cold cans of soda and a large, rich cake that had lots and lots of icing. The plan had been to serve everyone in the choir room, but there were so many people, including members of the prison choir, that it just wouldn't work. I looked up at the communion table, and said to myself, what would Jesus do? Then I sent two of the women to bring in the cake. When I am old and feeble, I will close my eyes and remember the scene that sent shivers to my heart. The officers had lined up the inmates — we had decided to let them go first because they were the ones who needed the cake — and in a stereotypical communion line, they processed up the aisle and up the steps to the altar-like table, two by two, to receive on a napkin a hunk of cake and to snatch a can of soda from the bucket that stood on the floor. As the line moved forward, one of the women waiting in the pew touched my arm and said to me, "Isn't this eucharist with a small 'e,' just like in your book?" Indeed, I had first mentioned small "e" eucharist in *The Singer and the Song*. I said to her, "Yes, it is." Then another women in the front of the chapel who had not heard this exchange, said, "This is like eucharist, like you wrote in your book." Remembering this brings tears to my eyes, for this was precisely what eucharist with a small "e" is all about, and incarcerated women were the first to see it. I was in prison and you visited me.

The spirit of Jesus was present there, grabbing a can of soda and carving up the cake.

Now that I have gotten started, there are a whole string of stories just waiting to be told. I will not have time to tell them here, but I do want to say that once we are in a storytelling mode, it is a lot harder to stop than it had been for us to begin. Right now I am remembering my mom and a number of stories related to food. In those last years before she died, we spent time in the kitchen where she showed me how to cook those meals I remembered from my childhood, sharing recipes she had never written down but kept carefully in her heart. She loved oatmeal for breakfast, and her idea of earthly bliss was to sit at my kitchen table and eat a bowl of oatmeal that I had prepared for her. After she died I asked her to come and visit me sometime, once she had gotten adjusted to the other side. Nothing sensational, I told her, just a brief moment in a dream, so I would know she was okay. Time passed, and then one night, as I was drifting off to sleep, I saw her face for an instant, as clear as if she were in the room, her wide eyes looking straight at me. She said one word to me. *Oatmeal!* And then she slipped away. I eat oatmeal most mornings. The box reminds me it is good for my heart, and indeed it is, because deep inside I am certain that I do this in memory of her.

So many of us have stories that are needing to be told. At the heart of eucharist with a small "e" is listening to those stories and then discerning together the nugget of wisdom or the flicker of inspiration that might be applicable to all. I interrupted my writing one day to have lunch with my friend, Donna, who is an advocate for the underclass and a much loved Jewish rabbi. When our meal arrived we joined hands and said a simple prayer, blessing our food, blessing each other, blessing all suffering people. For one brief moment, a small, crowded, noisy diner known locally as Mo's had become a sacred place. Our time together, from beginning to end, was small "e" eucharist. Now that is a story Jesus would tell, of two people sharing eucharist, a Christian and a Jew.

~ 17 ~

Sabbath

I will give thanks.
I will sing praise,
with all of my heart,
all of my days.

Sunday. First day of the week. Eighth day. Day of resurrection. It was first-century Christians who decided to keep holy the day when Christ rose from the dead.

The emergence of a Sabbath tradition coincides with the development of the Eucharist. Daily meals at home evolved to a meal with a ritual component and then a ritual minus the meal celebrated once a week on Sunday. The practice of keeping the Sabbath continued into modern times. Then malls and commercial enterprises pushing rampant consumerism claimed the day for themselves. Socioeconomic developments also made it necessary for single mothers, and for families where both parents had to work, to "get things done" on Sunday — shop, clean, wash the car, fix things up around the house — because that was the only time the busy household had to spare.

I remember Sunday as a child. There were things you could do and things you couldn't, because it was the Sabbath. I loved having time after church to write poems, read the funnies, color, and play with paper dolls. We always had chicken for dinner and Dad with us at the table, a special treat because troopers slept at the state police barracks several nights a week. I remember complaining about not being able to knit or sew or embroider, because that was considered work, which was forbidden on the Sabbath. Stitches sewn on Sunday would have to be removed in purgatory and would take nearly forever. Somebody had told my mother that, and she passed it on to me. The Sabbath was not for having fun or for doing what we wanted. It called for some serious reflecting. Remember, Jesus died for you, so act appropriately. Refrain from manual labor and spend some time in prayer. The Sabbath mood in those days was somber and restrictive, which put it on a collision course with a resurrection spirit. This may be one of the reasons why the keeping of the Sabbath has pretty much disappeared. Marketplace pressures provided an excuse to give it up and walk away.

The Christian tradition of a day set apart from our ordinary activities was influenced by the Jewish Shabbat, a weekly practice inspired by the first creation myth in Genesis, where God brought forth the world in six days, and on the seventh, rested. Six days in which to work. One day to refrain from working. To forgo those activities whereby we exercise control over the ordering of our lives is to restore a right relationship with God who created us and sustains us. It is a systemic acknowledgment that everything belongs to God. Down through the centuries this Jewish observance has been and still is sacred time, holy time, when essential personal and family rhythms are refreshed, renewed, and restored.

I believe in Sabbath time. I believe in Sabbath blessings. For Christians the interconnectedness of Sabbath, Eucharist, and the risen Christ is much too precious to lose. Our hectic, driven lives need the spiritual pause that refreshes and reorders priorities. However, what I will speak about here is not the Sunday Sabbath or the Sacrament of the Eucharist, but sabbath with a small "s" and its inherent relationship to eucharist with a small "e."

We return to the same creation story in the first chapter of Genesis, where God is active for six days and takes a break on the seventh. God begins by creating light and every day adds something new to the emerging cosmos. Over the course of five more days, God rearranges the waters; brings forth dry land with fruit-bearing trees and seed-bearing vegetation; adds day and night and the seasons; fills the waters with aquatic life and the skies above with birds; makes animals of every species, and then humans, female and male. When the work of creation is finished, God rests on the seventh day. Our sabbath rest relates to a pause in God's creative process, and so our sabbath differs from what is done on other days. However, what if we say that sabbath is integral to every day. This perspective is congruent with the Genesis text.

Consider the six days of creation not as a series of successive events in which life comes forth piece by piece, but a lifting up, one day at a time, of one of life's essentials, to allow us to focus on what really matters in the complex world around us, so we might remember not to take God's life-giving gifts for granted, so we realize that what we cherish most comes to us from God. Light and its affiliates in a cosmic dance with darkness; water, land, our precious planet, and all that dwells upon it. Remember, this is God's creation, so give God thanks and praise. The wisdom of the seventh day is not to pause for one day only, but to look for sabbath moments in any and every day. Just as created light was not limited to the first day but was meant to enlighten all our days, so too the sabbath principle is to sanctify every day. God's creation is continuous, day after day after day, and sabbath, integral to creation, weaves its way through all our days to remind us that this too is sacred time and sacred space.

From the chaotic way our worlds evolve we realize that creation is an evolutionary process that takes place every day. Sabbath reminds us daily that today is the day that God has made, so be grateful and be glad. We keep the sabbath when we take time to appreciate the world around us, when we pause to be mindful that life is sacred, that every day is holy, that everything comes from God. What we do to make a living, what it takes to make a house a home, the fulfillment of our responsibility as members of the human species to ensure the survival and the well-being of all creation, are precious in God's eyes. We do the work of God each day and daily we keep sabbath when we take time to ask God to sanctify our work and every aspect of our lives.

There is an integral relationship between eucharist with a small "e" and our reimagined sabbath. Both flow from a common Spirit and share a common ethos. Both witness to a resurrected hope and to a firm conviction that life itself belongs to God, and therefore, life is sacred. To those who celebrate small "e" eucharist, every day is holy. The very act of celebrating constitutes sabbath, declaring this space, this time, these people holy and blessed.

~ 18 ~

Spirit

All around
and deep within the world
Your all-pervading Spirit
manifests
Your power and Your presence,
Your life, Your love.

In the beginning, God. Creative and creating Spirit within the chaotic and limitless void imagines and all is made manifest. An outpouring of purposeful unpredictability. What was, is, and potentially will be forms within a dynamic web of inner-connectedness. Creative energy fills all that has visibility in the vastness of invisibility. Energy is Spirit, and Spirit is God.

The life force of the Spirit is the essence of existence. The breath of life, *ruach*, an image of the Spirit, is forever permeating, penetrating, perpetuating all. God fashions a human being from earth, or so the story goes, and breathes life into the one newly formed and into everyone ever after. We are all one in Spirit, for we inhale, exhale, share the living Spirit's breath of life. Sometimes our spirit becomes so brittle that the life force within begins to dry up. If left unattended, it dies.

Our spirits are revivified whenever we call on the Spirit and breathe in the breath of life.

When have I felt that Spirit within me giving me new life? Often. Daily. But more intensely at certain times . . . at the foot of a mountain touching the sky . . . by the sea, in the surf, on sandy beaches of oceans all around the world . . . seeing snow settle soft and white, transforming the world around me . . . when walking barefoot through the grass . . . wading in a clear and shallow stream . . . in the wind in the trees with no one around . . . in the syncopated drumbeat of rain when a sudden storm arrives unannounced . . . in katydids and insect choirs in the shadows of a summer night . . . seeing fireflies click off and on . . . in the full moon rising . . . in the song of the mockingbird just before dawn . . . while watching chipmunks . . . feeding the birds . . . spending time with someone I love . . . in the shared spirit of female friends . . . when writing poems . . . or singing songs . . . when imagining and reimagining . . . while writing this book about "e"ucharist . . . when I walk at night in the dark.

Spirit is always calling to us. The call comes from outside of us and also from within us, to suggest we move in a new direction or to convince us to stay right where we are. Sometimes the call is urgent and comes before we are ready, committing us to God knows what and God knows for how long. We are led into the wilderness or enticed to step out unencumbered into the vast unknown. So what if we feel inadequate or were making other plans. Like Jesus in the desert, we are shown the world's priorities and then are seemingly left on our own to make appropriate choices. But we are never really alone, for Spirit is always with us, though we may be unaware of it.

Spirit takes initiative at the heart of our ambivalence, in the midst of our indecisiveness, from the depths of our complacency, and speaks strength into our weakness, purpose into our prayer.

What do we do when confronted with what is clearly God's agenda? We turn in spirit to Jesus in order to learn from him. Energized after his desert sojourn, he announced that the spirit of God was upon him, compelling him to proclaim a liberating word to the poor and oppressed. When we feel the spirit of God upon us, all we can do is go forward in faith and be ready to leave our comfort zone, for a journey in the Spirit involves the opening of our eyes. Before long we will discover that the Spirit is *both/and*, not *either/or*, which makes life more confusing, because it messes with our set categories of us and them, friends and strangers, those who have and those who do not, those we think have been justified and those we suspect will be damned. Suddenly, we who are called to serve are the ones in need of attention, the proverbial wounded healer, the broken who long to be whole. The cry of the Spirit is the cry of the poor, the oppressed, and the imprisoned, the anguished wail of the victim brutally violated and abused. It is also the cry of the self-indulgent aware of the need for redemption and the cruel despot hovering on the edge of the abyss. The cosmic cry is a cry for help, a groan from the depths of creation, as Spirit writhes in the pain of being delivered by bringing to birth. In the midst of all this suffering, the caress of the Spirit rejuvenates with a passion for possibilities, a ludicrous burst of unshakeable hope, and a joy that will not waver. Counselor, Advocate, Comforter: how blessed are we when we learn to recognize the manifold ways God's spirit is made manifest in our lives.

We live in a world of chaos. All that had been predictable is now in perpetual flux. We keep on trying to fix it, to go back to the way it was before, but that only pulls us deeper into a vortex of discontent. The way it was, was never that way, except to the dominant forces, but we refuse to see it. Dissident voices, alternative visions, marginal populations were silenced or otherwise stifled and kept under strict control. Existence is dynamic. The forces of nature are always churning. The goal is not equilibrium. To be in stasis is to be dead. We ache to hear prophetic voices heralding the future, pointing us in the direction of evolution and not extinction. Jesus was a prophetic voice channeling the Spirit, as so many did before him and so many do today. The challenge to closed systems, sociopolitical and religious, is to enter into the chaos as if it were a whirlpool of potentiality. Trust intuition, seek inspiration, evoke imagination, for this is the language Spirit speaks. Be prepared to hear it.

The times we live in call for a radical reorientation, not only of how we view our world, but how we behave within it. We cannot keep doing what we have always done, favor those groups who have always been favored, for the universe will not allow it. In many ways, it is rising up to befriend the disenfranchised, seeking justice on their behalf. We have a responsibility to pour into the matrix a transforming perspective. We are called to proclaim that the healing, wholesome, compassionate sensitivities of the Spirit are present everywhere and accessible to all. The primary lesson of Pentecost is that chaos is the Spirit's realm and, as such, is ripe with potential.

We need not cringe from chaos. Instead, we should welcome it as the creative and life-giving force of our Creator God.

Eucharist with a small "e" is an initiative of the Spirit that offers us opportunity to speak a liberating word and to practice what we proclaim. It nurtures a spirituality of access and accessibility, for the spirit of small "e" eucharist is the living spirit of Jesus, who is one with all whose spirits are longing to be whole. Spirit and ritual overlap in the word "spirituality," just as they overlap and intertwine in the living of our lives. Rituals of life that embody spirit define our life in the Spirit. Therefore, eucharist with a small "e" is rooted in rituals of Spirit that celebrate life.

Small "e" eucharist rituals, whether brief or more extended, form us and transform us, so that eventually our spirit, the spirit of Jesus, and the spirit of God within every facet of God's creation are really and truly one. Some are certain to ask: was the table fellowship of Jesus really eucharist? If the real, physical presence of the historical Jesus is not eucharist, I don't know what is. The very real spirit presence of Jesus at our own sacramental meals most certainly is.

Also by Miriam Therese Winter

The Singer and the Song
An Autobiography of the Spirit
ISBN 1-57075-279-6

190 pages, paperback

This spiritual memoir of a remarkable woman—musician, author, missionary—will inspire not only those who know her work but anyone interested in living a life of love and service.

"In this uplifting memoir, the four-time Catholic Book Award winner demonstrates how the Divine Musician has played grace notes through the words and deeds of her life....Winter consistently challenges us to reverence the activity of the Holy One within the precincts of everyday life."
—*Spirituality and Health*

Please support your local bookstore, or call 1-800-258-5838.
For a free catalogue, please write us at
Orbis Books, Box 308
Maryknoll NY 10545-0308
or visit our website at www.orbisbooks.com

Thank you for reading *eucharist with a small "e."*
We hope you enjoyed it.